WORKING WITH COMMUNITIES

Paul Henderson (Editor)

The Children's Society
London

First published in 1988 by
The Children's Society
Edward Rudolf House
Margery Street
London WC1X 0JL

British Library Cataloguing in Publication Data

Working with communities
    1. Great Britain. Community development
    I. Henderson, Paul, *1942-* II. Church of
    England, *Children's Society*
    307'.14'0941
    ISBN 0 907324 32 0

Typeset by Infograph Ltd
Printed and bound in Great Britain by Thameside Printers

Contents

Foreword

From the Bishop of Stepney, The Rt Rev Jim Thompson

Working with Communities is a valuable series of articles which could be read and studied with profit by both the Church and the wider community. I found there a helpful analysis of the great issues we have been facing in the last ten years. There is so much in common between this thinking and the developing understanding of those parts of the Church which live out the sort of care described. The debate is going on in Boards for Social Responsibility, in social services, in the voluntary sector. It is my belief that these are important rumblings, and they represent the sound of the mainstream of local care.

These questions, however, are not just for the professionals or interested volunteers, but for all those involved in the debate about the nature of the Welfare State, the quality of life, the mutual responsibility we all have for society as a whole. I don't like to think how many times in my own ministry I have argued that more resources should be put into prevention rather than into what we used to think of as the 'hospital' approach. If we concentrate on mending or replacing children's teeth, we produce generations of decaying teeth. If we concentrate our resources on prevention, we produce healthier teeth and cut the overall dental bill. As a team in a new town, we used to be shown architectural plans and we used to say "they look like Gestapo headquarters – build them and you will increase the neuroses and turn healthy people into sick, dependent people". There are examples of good practice where local people are properly involved, the latent strength of our communities is built upon, and opportunities are created for local people to grow in responsibility and therefore quality of life. This collection of articles works out, on the basis of pioneering experience, the way in which this movement affects children and families.

This leads on to fundamental questions about our society, our values and our sense of purpose. This will not be an easy arena in which to speak and listen. There is a famous saying of Dom Helda Camara – "When I fed the hungry, they called me a saint – when I asked why they were hungry, they called me a Marxist". The family is rightly at the centre of much debate, and children are most at risk when the family is broken. The family is often broken where a poor environment, despair about the future and sharp deprivation prevail. It is not possible to call a halt at the question about the individual family without asking in addition the question about the context and the injustice.

It is a source of hope that The Children's Society and the Church should be asking the same questions and trying to tackle many of the same issues. This should be a great encouragement and inspiration for us. At its best, the parish church should be a neighbourhood centre, with links in the community, which has as a priority the prevention of family breakdown, the creation of a good quality of life and the provision of a source of strength and security for children. It is to be hoped that the churches will continue to be one of the main outlets for the developments which will follow from these articles. I hope that our institution will be as open and prepared for change as The Children's Society will have to be if the ideas are to be resourced, supported and developed. I hope many people will read this helpful and stimulating vision.

Acknowledgements

For most people, writing is an uphill task. When doing it alongside other work the enterprise can appear daunting. I am full of admiration, therefore, for the contributors to this publication for maintaining their commitment. The results spring directly from current practice and experience.

I am also grateful to Mary Jean Pritchard (Publications Editor) and Ruth Hall (Consultant) of The Children's Society for their support in this collaborative project. Their personal and professional concern has been invaluable.

It is gratifying that The Children's Society considered the subect matter of sufficient importance to put resources into the publication. That augurs well.

Paul Henderson
Editor

INTRODUCTION

Paul Henderson

The end of the 1980s may see social work being forced in one of two directions: towards the delivery of selective services, geared in the main to protecting children, or towards a community approach whereby work with clients is integrated with support for informal networks and community groups. At present, the profession is poised between the two. Public, media and some political pressures are pushing it in the first direction; ideas and experience within the profession itself, and political pressures favouring voluntarism and community care, push it towards the second. It is incorrect to equate the first approach with control and the second exclusively with care, yet those people practising and teaching community social work are frequently reminded of the vulnerability of a community approach because it is seen to deflect attention from direct work with clients.

This collection of articles falls firmly within the community-based approach to social work. I believe that the articles relate to a community social work framework, and I intend to explain what this is and how the articles can be read from this perspective. First, however, it is necessary to put the collection in the context of the work of The Children's Society.

Organisational context

The decision of The Children's Society, towards the end of the 1970s, to encourage and support the development of family centres was an important watershed. As Jan Phelan explains in her study of family centres, the Society began to see children and their welfare in terms of the neighbourhoods in which they lived: "the Society became increasingly involved in community and neighbourhood based approaches, even though it was a marginal activity and somewhat tentative".[1] The development of the decentralised regional structure has been important in pushing forward family centres and a neighbourhood approach, with projects and staff also receiving support from headquarters' staff.

The underlying philosophy behind these changes, which historically will be seen as profoundly significant for the Society, is the idea of prevention within a community setting; prevent ill-treatment of children, prevent children being taken into care. Between 1981 and 1987 these ideas have provided the justification behind the continual development of family centres and the expansion of work in neighbourhoods, neither of which can now be said to be marginal or tentative within the Society. Some, indeed, wish to take the prevention argument further – to move from the negative connotation of prevention to the idea of promotion of quality of life, and to notions of empowerment of clients, users and local people.

The Society's staff – in projects and in regional offices – have not held back from exploration and articulation of community-based forms of practice. Bob Holman, who initiated the Southdown Project in Bath, has written of the advantages of the approach.[2] Other staff have been actively involved with initiatives to establish firmer guidelines for community social work practice. In the North West Region, for example, the Society convened early meetings of a community social work network aimed at involving staff from a range of voluntary and statutory agencies. Other evidence of the interest in strengthening community practice is the links project staff have made with community workers and their organisations. For example, staff in the Wales and West of England Region are involved in a national study of the relevance to the UK of training institutions in the USA which use the methods of the celebrated community organiser Saul Alinsky.

If community social work is firmly on the agendas of the Society's fieldworkers and regional staff, how is it viewed by headquarters' staff and Council members? In 1981 the Society's constitution was changed to facilitate work in communities. Two years later the Director appointed a working party on community involvement and local control, and its report[3] addresses the major practice and policy issues facing the Society. The report aroused widespread interest within the Society, and in 1986 the new Director set up a working group to consider the responses of staff. This group's report focuses on the practical implications of a local control policy.

To the outsider, there is no evidence to suggest that headquarters' staff or Council and committee members are resistant to the Society taking further its work in communities. It is legitimate to ask whether they are resistant, however, because the main thrust towards community involvement is coming from the projects and the regions.

The Society's move from being essentially a specialist child care agency to being a community agency which has a social work brief with a particular concern for children clearly has implications for the organisation, including its appeals staff. The organisation is aware of this, and is seeking to address the issues which the change is raising.

For the future historian of the Society, part of the fascination will lie in tracing the extent to which a number of other child care organisations also moved towards community social work during this period: Barnardo's, National Children's Home, Save the Children Fund. The pace and approach of each organisation varies, but together they fit a pattern. I have tried to highlight the key developments in the case of The Children's Society, but other causes will be found within the values of society as a whole, and are likely to turn upon the following three themes:

(a) Christianity and community

The search for community is on the agendas of Christian churches in Britain, and it takes a number of forms. There is a strong theological interest, with thinkers like Margaret Kane[4] and the Bishop of Durham putting forward ideas in ways which make theology accessible to a much wider spectrum of believers. Christian leaders have also been more willing to challenge the relevance of Christian practice and institutions to issues such as poverty and deprivation – especially in the inner city. In the Anglican Church the Bishop of Liverpool's *Bias to the Poor*[5] was followed by the Archbishop's commission's report *Faith in the City*[6]: both contain powerful messages. Other denominations have shown a similar concern to address urgent social issues. These and other developments, which I have space only to mention here, must certainly have permeated and influenced The Children's Society. Christian belief and commitment has been, and remains, so central to the life of the Society that it would be surprising if this had not been so. A reading of relevant documents, such as the draft statement on Society philosophy (1984), provides evidence of how the Society has been part of the search by Christian churches and organisations to respond more effectively to the inequalities and injustices in British society, to make itself more relevant to the lives of ordinary people in parishes and neighbourhoods.

(b) Social and economic conditions

There can be little doubt that the Society's involvement in community social work is in part a response to its experience and analysis of social and economic conditions. When the lives and the expectations of whole sections of the country's population are overturned by structural unemployment, economic decline and an array of social problems, social work agencies must surely re-examine how they work in communities. They face issues which are common to large numbers of people in neighbourhoods and which threaten to undermine many of the resources within those neighbourhoods.

Agencies have to respond to the social effects of major economic changes, however unclear their relationship with the agency is: poverty, family break-up, increased crime rates, and the psychological impact of being part of a community which is experiencing powerlessness. The inner city riots of 1981 and 1985 were dramatic manifestations of deeply felt feelings within communities, and they were events which agencies could hardly ignore. Furthermore, agencies could not fail to measure less visible evidence of social deprivation and injustice.

Through various channels – its membership, research reports, fieldworkers, local churches – the Society is well placed to receive a constant flow of data on social deprivation. It has made use of these data to re-work its strategies and make decisions on where it will place its social work and community work resources.

Increasingly these decisions have been directed at providing a response at community level, in co-operation with other agencies and with local people.

(c) Social policy

Soon after the Conservatives came to power in 1979, government ministers began to advocate the advantages of mobilising informal carers, volunteers and self-help groups. At one point it seemed as if the functions of social services departments were to be pared down to the minimum, with extra resources being put into the voluntary sector. The government has drawn back from this. However, it still intends to support community care policies, even if the delivery of them remains unsatisfactory.[7]

This feature of social policy has had its effect on voluntary organisations. I am referring both to the programmes on offer from the government's Manpower Service Commission (eg, Opportunities for Volunteering) and to dominant ideas. Erica De'Ath has traced the inter-connections between self help and family centres during this period,[8] and it can be argued that the Society's espousal of family centres within the neighbourhood context is consistent at a policy level with the government's interest in voluntary organisations as vehicles for its community care policies.

Equally, at local government level, the Society may, in many instances, be knocking at an open door: social services departments which are experiencing the dual pressures of providing an effective child care service and making more use of informal networks may turn to the Society – or to other voluntary organisations – with a sense of relief. It can be a way for social services departments to hand over some of the planning and pilot work entailed.

The foregoing analysis may not stand up to rigorous examination, but then all social policy concerned with care in the community is notoriously intangible. At the very least one can pose the question: is the Society's interest in community social work inspired solely by its own values and policies, or is it being led to some extent by a combination of social policy 'ideas in the wind' and the possibility of resources? The Society, in other words, may be a consumer or victim of social policy as well as contributor to it.

Clearly the Society is concerned to monitor the effects of certain social policies on communities. Often the effects are unanticipated – for example, the impact on families of people in areas of high unemployment searching for jobs in more economically buoyant regions. Thus the recent creation at headquarters of a social policy department is a significant development. Interestingly, most of the other major voluntary child care organisations can be seen to be strengthening their social policy work too. It suggests a growing concern to examine the reasons behind the continuing existence of severe social problems.

I have identified the Christian concern with community, social and economic conditions, and aspects of contemporary social policy as important themes underlying the Society's concern with community social work. These themes are offered tentatively, and they can certainly be added to. What is important is to retain this external perspective on the Society's development, to debate how far the internal processes of the organisation, in addition to being managed by members, committees and staff, are also shaped by forces operating throughout society. This consideration applies equally powerfully to a discussion of community social work.

Community social work

Several models of community social work practice have emerged over the past ten years and they vary according to organisational and community setting. East Sussex Social Services Department, for example, has developed a model from a departmental policy decision to decentralise services, while in other large agencies a particular approach has been identified with only one or two teams. The probation team covering the Gipton estate and part of Harehills in Leeds, for example, has evolved a form of community-based practice which is not found in most other teams in the city.

The shape of the practice will also be determined by the values of the staff concerned, either individually or as a team. I would like to offer some ideas on this; they do not purport to be a theory, nor are they concerned with the organisation and resourcing of community social work. Rather they seek to capture the central themes which, in my opinion, sustain community social work in the Society's projects – the motivating forces which inform practice in a very direct way. The ideas themselves are not original, but they signal – as much by the language used as by the content – the style and approach of community social work. It is important for community social work to retain its freshness and energy, which is why the language used becomes critical.

The reader may wish to reflect on the relationship between continuity and change. The ideas outlined below do not represent Children's Society policy, but they cannot be seen as separate from the values which have been at the centre of the Society's work for a long time. In a sense, the tensions between the four themes of the following framework – especially between the first and second – mirror debates and reflections within the Society.

(a) Working to strengths

A social worker or community worker who becomes part of a depressed or alienated community risks becoming professionally disabled. The worker has to maintain hope and optimism that situations and people can change; in a sense, he or she has to retain a certain naivety. It is important to emphasise that working in and with communities is people-focused and draws the worker or project away from being obsessively problem-focused. Of course, community social work addresses people's problems, but it does so through working with people to identify the problems of a neighbourhood or community of interest, prioritising the problems and working out a strategy for tackling them. This can mean that the starting point is not problem-focused at all.

The milieu or setting for community social work therefore has to be the community or neighbourhood where people live and interact. The community social work team has to become accepted and trusted by people and groups in the neighbourhood. It will remain external to the neighbourhood, because its staff are accountable elsewhere and because its staff usually differ from local people in their education and social class, and frequently their race. They should, however, still be able to win the trust of local people.

A wide variety of methods is available to such workers to help them achieve the crucial objective of gaining trust. Social workers need to be familiar with these methods and test them out. They also have to become accustomed to working in an open environment, in the sense that they cannot control all the factors which determine what they do. In my experience, some social workers find this attitude difficult to accept; this reflects the training and job remits of social workers, not the individuals themselves. Social workers tend to feel responsible for all activities which come within their orbit. It is important that they break free from this. At one level this means social workers having to tolerate greater uncertainty – not blaming themselves, for example, if a group starts to dwindle. At another level it means having to address two fundamental principles:

– Social workers do not have a monopoly of social work. Care and control; help for relatives, friends and neighbours; mutual aid take place – often in modest, unassuming ways – in all communities. Social workers need to be skilled at recognising these acts of human concern, and, furthermore, need to work with them.

– Community social work assumes the existence or possibility of community responsibility for social problems. This element of empowerment within community social work says: social work agencies are seeking to work more closely with communities, not only because this will make their work more effective, but also because they believe that communities have to take back some of the care and control functions which the agencies thought they could undertake on behalf of communities.

This is a difficult theme to advance because of its ambiguity. Does it mean that communities are being thrown back onto a crude form of self-help, rationed to a limited amount of help from external agencies? Or does it reflect a libertarian stream which says that ordinary people have the capacity to take responsibility on social matters, and they should be given more opportunities to do so? Wherever one puts oneself in that debate, some theory of community responsibility is contained within the philosophy of community social work which takes seriously the notion of strength and resources of local people. The issue is to reverse the relationship of dependency which has evolved between communities and agencies.

(b) A focus on individuals

Social work methods have tended to focus on work with individuals, usually on a one-to-one basis. Community social work, by implication, seeks to broaden the range of methods available to social workers – but for what purpose?

Methods need to be distinguished from goals. It is dangerously misleading to suggest that community social work seeks always to organise people on the basis of a shared need, problem, or issue into groups. I would argue that, certainly at this stage in the development of community social work, the opposite meaning should be assumed: community social work aims to respond to the needs of individuals and families in their communities.

The methods and strategies used to achieve this will undoubtedly include community work, and a project or team is likely to need to include one or more community workers, but essentially a community social work approach is concerned with the wellbeing of individuals. I am advocating, therefore, a strong distinction between community social work and community work, for the aim of the latter is not focused primarily on the individual.

It is important to be aware that the focus on work with individuals can take place in several contexts. For example, it can form part of an analysis of users of a family centre – why particular individuals become involved in groups or activities over different periods of time. It should also be an important criterion for a team's constituency of interest and support: the team is not a tenants' association, whose potential constituency would be all tenants on an estate, it is a group of professional staff whose constituency includes a range of individuals whom they are in a position to help. The Society's over-riding concern is for the welfare and development of children and families, and it is this which can provide the framework of the Society's commitment to community social work.

(c) Participation

A participatory model of practice is a key principle in

community social work – participation of staff in agencies' decision-making processes, and participation of users and other local people in the work of a team or project. This model also assumes that priority is given to working closely with other agencies or projects. When taken seriously – ie, when taken beyond a token interest, the theme of participation in community social work has major implications for the structuring and resourcing of a team. At the very least it would imply monitoring the extent and types of participation, but that would be a very limited recognition of the issue. Evidence suggests that staff have to work hard at finding ways of getting people involved, and there are many, well documented techniques for doing this. What have to underpin their use, however, are: firstly, a reasonably coherent philosophy as to why participation is so crucial; secondly, the necessary resources – in particular, the time and skills of workers – to put it into practice.

(d) Giving and taking
Community social work must involve an open partnership between agencies and communities. Agencies must learn that communities hold certain forms of power and influence and cannot be treated simply as a 'resource' which has to inform community social work practice. There is a moral side to this argument – namely, that it is wrong to use or exploit human resources without giving something in return. There is also a more practical point: that local resources will cease to respond to the demands of agencies unless the agencies reciprocate; local people would either become unwilling to co-operate with agencies, or would actually start to challenge them.

The principle that professionals need to find ways of giving their time and skills to help local people, or making a case for more resources for a neighbourhood, has major implications for the planning and resourcing of teams. The biggest challenge of this approach is that it implies that staff will at times have to work on the terms of a local group rather than their agency's terms.

Testing situations can arise. For example, if the committee of a neighbourhood centre seeks to exclude particular individuals from the centre on the grounds that they are 'unsuitable' when there is no evidence of this unsuitability – what does a staff team do? They may debate the matter with the committee, but there could come a point when either they are forced to make a stand, thereby alienating the committee, or they agree to the committee having its way. If they do this, have they reneged on their values, or have they respected the right of local people to have different values? What is clear is that professionals' values will have to stand alongside those of local people; they cannot be assumed.

The theme of giving is at the centre of Christian belief, and is wholly consonant with The Children's Society's values. It is particularly important to remember that service is central to the lives of Christians because of the changes within the churches referred to earlier. The re-awakening of the Church to the issues of poverty, deprivation and unemployment is significant for The Children's Society and its work with communities through its projects and centres. Not only does this provide some context for the Society's work; it also provides a moral and spiritual cutting edge for the Society to intervene actively in communities by sharing its resources, ideas, knowledge and skills with local people.

The last of my four community social work themes serves to remind us that both internal and external observers of the Society's work are right to look for distinctive characteristics. Developments in community social work are taking place within social services departments, probation services and other voluntary organisations. Each organisational setting will influence the kind of practice which emerges. Those agencies and individuals who are sharing experiences and ideas about community social work practice on a regional basis have to be aware of this: while they search together for common theories and practice they do so in the knowledge that these will need to be re-worked to fit with the particular philosophy and structures of their agency. The evidence suggests to me – and it is supported by this collection of articles – that the Society is fulfilling the classic function of a voluntary organisation – namely, pioneering new forms of practice, and testing long-held assumptions. It is not alone in this; other voluntary organisations are also contributing in this way to the thinking of statutory agencies. In what ways do the articles in this collection demonstrate that the Society is making a distinctive contribution?

References

1 Phelan J. *Family Centres – A Study*. London: The Children's Society, 1983.

2 Holman R. *Resourceful Friends – Skills in Community Social Work*. London: The Children's Society, 1983.

3 Working party. *Local control*. London: The Children's Society, 1984.

4 Kane M. *What Kind of God?* London: SCM Press,1986.

5 Sheppard D. *Bias to the Poor*. London: Hodder and Stoughton, 1983.

6 Archbishop of Canterbury's Commission. *Faith in the City*. London: Church House, 1985.

7 Audit Commission. *Report*. 1986.

8 De'Ath E. *Self Help and Family Centres*. London: National Children's Bureau, 1985.

THE ARTICLES

Firstly, however, we need to ask how the articles relate to the framework of ideas outlined above. Are there common ideas running through all the contributions? Do they together reflect developments and ideas within The Children's Society, or are we grasping for form and consistency where none exist? Readers will make up their own minds on these issues, but they may be helped if I signpost some themes which I think emerge.

First, *community development* has a dominant presence in several of the articles. Many staff employed to work in family centres and neighbourhood projects do not have social work backgrounds. They may have been trained as youth and community workers and practised as detached youth workers or community development officers before joining the Society. They may find it difficult to relate to a community social work framework despite being employed by a social work agency.

This sense that some fieldworkers feel a strong allegiance to community development values and methods is evident in the articles by Joe Hasler, Rosie Edwards and Neil Proctor/Jenny Sayer. The aims of the work described relate strongly to the theme of working to the strengths of local people. The articles might equally appear in a collection of community work articles as in a Children's Society publication.

Yet work with children and families remains a thread running through all the papers, even those with the strongest orientation towards community development. Thus Neil Proctor and Jenny Sayer note that the original proposal for the South Bank Project contained a clearly identified community development approach "working alongside and with families and groups in the community, rather than with families on a treatment basis."

Perhaps it is not surprising that holding the two themes of community development and work with children and families within one project's framework can sometimes give rise to difficulties. The Millmead Project, about which Rosie Edwards writes, is surely not alone in experiencing a tension between four elements: activities, resources, individuals and alliances.

This issue alerts us to a second theme emerging from the articles: *concern for the organisation*. While I hold that the authors face predominantly in the direction of grassroots activities and teamwork, they also display an awareness that they work for a national voluntary organisation which not only has its own history, aims and values, but which also has to function as a total organisation: decision-making processes at national, regional and local levels (involving committee members at national level as well as staff); an appeals section; and other necessary components of a national body such as publicity and publications.

The Social Work Division of the Society has six regions. Each region is managed by a team of approximately six staff and has between twelve and fifteen projects. In short, the Society has evolved an hierarchical system of organisation, a system of which project staff are aware and in which they participate.

I suspect, however, that the actual community work practice of project staff has the effect of drawing them away from the organisation. Indeed, one would wish to ask some questions if this were not so: the language of partnership and participation contains significant implications for how project staff carry out their roles, and this may be an area of practice and policy with which the Society will have to grapple (see last article 'Looking Forward').

One effect is to underline the skills needed by the Society's middle managers, particularly the assistant regional directors, because they must have acute understanding of the style and aspirations of projects and at the same time be good at communicating the dynamics and tensions of projects both to senior management colleagues and to their counterparts in social services departments and other agencies with which they negotiate.

The *planning implications* for the Society of developing community projects is a third theme which can be identified within several of the articles. This is explicit in some (see part 2), and implicit in others – Celia Burn's description of change occurring in the Derbyshire Hill project over an eight year period, for example. Three issues which need to be faced in the planning context are: user and community involvement in projects; the degree to which projects aim to include a strong inter-agency element in their work; and evaluation.

A fourth theme which strikes the reader sharply is how much of the work described is being done, in *neighbourhoods experiencing a range of economic and social pressures.* This, it can be said, is a statement of the obvious: as Peter Wiggin notes in his paper, the Society's enquiries prior to setting up a project will focus on areas which have high indicators of social need. At least six of the projects described in this publication are located on council estates. These tend to be 'labelled', stressful communities which survive on a threadbare local economy with high unemployment rates and a plethora of social problems. It is in these kinds of areas that the Society's projects tend to be located.

In addition to being aware of the extent to which projects are working in these kinds of neighbourhoods, the reader may wish to reflect on the following questions:

Do staff who are working in these areas need to receive additional forms of support if they are not to 'burn-out' after about two years?

How will the Society be perceived by potential sponsors and host organisations if the tendency to work in 'problem areas' continues? Does the Society feel happy at being part of a rescue strategy by local authorities for their most problematic neighbourhoods?

Will there be implications for projects' relationships with local people and users if the equation between the Society's work and certain kinds of neighbourhoods solidifies? How eager will people be to become involved if a project is seen to have been set up to deal with 'their' problems, especially when they discover that other projects of the Society are in a similar mould?

Finally, if the Society believes it is right to concentrate its resources on identified problem neighbourhoods, is it doing enough at a policy level to analyse the outcomes of the work of projects? Is it using the learning which is accumulating about how to work in such neighbourhoods both to improve its own policy making and to inform other agencies and government? Can one see a stronger advocacy role for the Society as being the logical outcome of its increased involvement in local communities?

The wider political context is the final theme I wish to identify. It is not addressed strongly in the articles. Authors were asked to focus on their experiences rather than engage in political analysis. One is aware, however, of the political context, in terms of, firstly, the pressures on neighbourhoods referred to above, and, secondly, the role being played by the Society. Over the past eight years public expenditure has been reduced, drastically so in the case of public housing; the quality of life on estates where many of the Society's projects are located is declining as a result of social policies. High levels of unemployment, inadequate maintenance of the housing stock, and clear evidence of increased family poverty are the most obvious manifestations of decline. There is a need for projects such as those of the Society to respond to these situations. Accordingly we have a voluntary organisation, in some instances carrying 100 per cent of the project costs, working with neighbourhoods whose fragmentations and depressions are partly the result of government policies. What is more, the thrust of projects is to encourage local people to take on more community responsibilities: self-help as a response to despair and reduced resources.

This crude equation is put forward in simple terms in order to highlight the fine line which the Society treads as projects move towards community involvement and local control. Most staff will be aware of the issues. It is important to re-state them here, however, in order to emphasise the wider political climate in which projects are working. They are not islands of activity, cut off from powerful currents which are in danger of eroding the very lands where they are based! If a middle manager senses that a project is totally inward-looking, wholly caught up in its involvement with one neighbourhood, then I think that he or she has to find ways of alerting project staff to the external forces and influences which are impinging directly on that neighbourhood. The same, of course, applies in reverse: project staff need to insist that regional and national staff pick up the policy implications of their work.

The political dimension of the Society's community involvement policies must surely represent a challenge rather than an embarrassment. It suggests the need for informed discussion and clear thinking. This is particularly the case when government funding is available for projects which the Society could mount. It is all too easy for the balance between an organisation reaching decisions on the basis of its values and priorities, plus awareness of funding availability, to be skewed towards the latter, especially when there is growing evidence of severe social need. This danger, of course, exists for many other organisations besides The Children's Society.

There are also more general issues relating to community projects and community social work which are raised by the articles which follow. In the last part of the book, the Director of The Children's Society examines some of these from the point of view of the Society, and I share some general concluding comments.

The other chapters have been placed in two sections, each of which is preceded by a short linking passage. This may facilitate use of the book, allowing readers to select particular parts and chapters depending on their interest.

PART 1 – FAMILIES AND COMMUNITY DEVELOPMENT

The articles in this first section stay close to the day-to-day activities of Society staff who are developing neighbourhood-based family and children's work. They are 'nuts and bolts' articles, allowing the outside observer to catch a glimpse of what is involved in this kind of practice.

Few writers address directly the interconnections between community development and child care. Joe Hasler does so through a combination of critical questioning and reflection on his estate-based community work experience. He asks the reader to consider the total environment of the child. There is an implicit challenge to community work here, in that work with children has often been seen primarily as a means to an end: the summer playscheme or the community playgroup, while providing valued activities for children, can be a way of mobilising adults in an area. Joe Hasler's conclusion, on the other hand, would turn child care and development into a more central objective for some community projects. His arguments, therefore, will be of interest to child care agency policy-makers as well as to practitioners.

Celia Burn identifies a number of issues which arise between the Society and a community group when there is a close partnership between the two at local level. As a result she touches upon the implications for the Society of a local control policy. It is interesting to note, in particular, how her role changed to being more of a consultant – and how this was equally time-consuming. The work described by Celia Burn can also be compared with the first article in terms of the focus on children and families.

The same issue is contained in the contribution by Rosie Edwards. We see how work with children and families becomes integrated with a variety of community activities. People are encouraged to take the 'first step' towards becoming involved with others for a variety of reasons and motives. The more that a project can plan for this the more likely it is to be effective. There will still be planning and priority problems for staff, but these will be located in 'a clear community development approach.' The project described by Rosie Edwards contains lessons for both the Society and other organisations seeking to develop community-based practice.

The enigmatic title of Liam Condron's article signals the tensions which can exist in community work. In this instance the main area of tension is between a local project seeking to work with people in an identified community and a special project ready to work on a town-wide basis. The writing demonstrates the effects of this 'pull' and provides an honest account of the energy which exists in good community projects. The skills and priorities of staff are challenged and buffeted by local opinion. The article identifies the elements of a 'turbulent marriage' without conveying negative messages.

In their different ways all four studies touch upon the professional implications for project staff of community-based work. The full import of these have still to be clarified within the Society. The articles which follow suggest a number of areas which require close analysis. They offer 'live material' from which to work. If they are read with the role of the worker in mind, this focus will be evident: what choices did he or she have in a particular situation? to what extent did he or she move between roles during the project's life? I am convinced that the discipline of concentrating on the details and specifics of practice in this way will help the Society to reach a better understanding of the professional implications of community-based practice.

COMMUNITY DEVELOPMENT – IS IT CHILD CARE?

Joe Hasler

Introduction

Community development usually means a process through which people in an area are encouraged to get together. They are helped to plan, decide, and act together about things that matter to them. Community workers claim that the people involved discover their own abilities. Furthermore, because they do so in a framework of common needs they and the community benefit.

The Children's Society has a long history of traditional social work. I have a background in community work and detached youth work. In talking to supporters and employees of The Children's Society about community work I find that there is a gap between their understanding and mine. I try to speak about community work as a partnership with parents, a partnership made in the interest of the child. I give examples of how people care for their own and other people's children, but I do not show how community work is required to do these things. The result is that I am still asked, "Where is the child care in all this community work?" I hope to address this question. First I will show how this question grows out of the traditional concerns of social work. I will also discuss children in community as well as community work.

I will try to say something about my own work, offering assorted thoughts, and details of events in which I have been involved. I will aim to choose stories and views that will ring true with others working in the field. These stories intend to show:

a) how it is that children find community;
b) how their families operate in communities I have known.

I will then try to point out three ways in which community development can achieve some aspects of child care. I believe that these aspects should be seen as equal in importance to others in child care.

The Children's Society – its social work history

The Children's Society had a long history of homefinding and children's homes. In the 1960s things began to change: there were fewer babies for adoption; fewer children were coming into residential care. Homefinding teams began helping children with special needs. Children's homes moved their focus towards therapy and rehabilitation. The work of the Society moved to take account of these changes. The Children's Society also became involved in family centres. Early advertisements for staff in family centres sought those who would work at the points where social work and community work meet. Thus community development became a key idea to The Children's Society.

These ideas were given weight by two changes in policy. Firstly, the Society wanted to work from the needs outwards. Secondly, the Society was beginning to accept that caring for the family meant caring for the community.

At that time community workers took 'Starting from the needs outwards' to mean needs that the clients define. Caring for families in the context of community was seen to be community work. With hindsight both these statements could have meant something else.

We can see that both these policies could have been interpreted differently. Social workers increasingly realise that they do not need to start from a base of traditional social work. One example of how workers have come to realise this is Bob Holman's book *Resourceful Friends*.[1] This book talks about the shortcomings of social work training for community work.

The history of social work is also reflected in the idea that care for the child in community must involve the family; we use the family as a buffer between the child and the community. This is because social workers have visited children in the homes of their parents, or substitute families, and it is from the home that social workers picture what goes

4

on. In fact, working with children in the community does not always require face-to-face contact with parents – children have a rich life outside of home and school. Traditionally, social work starts from the position of dealing with the child in its home.

I would like to explore the question of the child in the community from a starting point of the child in the street.

Child culture

"The scraps of lore that children learn from each other are at once more real, more immediately serviceable, and more vastly entertaining to them than anything they learn from grown-ups." This is the first sentence from *The Lore and Language of School Children* by Iona and Peter Opie,[2] a book which leaves you in no doubt that a child culture exists.

I have noticed that in those areas where large households of growing children are concentrated there seems to be a richer local children's culture. Maybe larger sibling groups make this culture more obvious to the community worker. In *Cycles of Disadvantage*[3] Rutter and Madge show that if a boy has been involved in delinquency there is a chance his brother will also become involved. This chance is in fact much more likely than the chances of a delinquent father having a delinquent son. This may indicate the strength of peer influences. In the area where we work some parents say: "No matter what you do you can see your children heading for trouble". In some respects these people can see that peer influences are stronger than those of the parent. Children's culture is given credibility by many people. Community workers have helped local people to create, and relate to, a range of play projects – eg, adventure playgrounds, children's clubs and detached youth work. Play and children's culture go hand-in-hand.

However, children's culture stands distant from the world of adults. It is esoteric; it has a local dimension; for the child it is real. In many senses it is the child's community. Incidentally, 'caring for the child in its own community' has come to mean that the child is better off in his/her own home than in a children's home. It means little more, and takes little account of children's culture.

Family in community on outer estates

My own community development work over the past 13 years has been on outer estates of mainly council-built houses. If I recall the surveys done on these estates, they have each asked if households have relatives living in other houses on the estate. The estates on which I have worked have varied in age and I have found that the number of related households goes up as the estates become more settled. The estate where I now work is 48 years old and you need to think twice before you gossip: I still notice the power of mother and daughter links. This means that the effect of family on community exchanges must be taken into account by community workers.

Traditionally, social work has developed a picture of the family from what is called the 'home visit'; its starting point is two parents and the children in a particular household. This is what is often referred to as 'the family'.

The place of family in the community takes on a new meaning when the poverty of the '80s is taken into account. Mass unemployment means people have more time and less money.

Community projects may promote activities for children such as pre-school playgroups, mothers and toddlers, holiday schemes. Local people may get involved in a variety of community programmes for little or no reward – why do local people volunteer for such activities? It is possible that altruism is alive. It is also likely that some form of exchange or reward is at work. A playgroup helper may only want news or gossip in exchange for their services; maybe they want babysitting for their own children, less often but at more anti-social times. P Abrahams indicates that the nature of the exchange may be complex but is never far away.[4]

I recall when two groups running one youth club – each with a strong extended family at its core – underwent a struggle for power. It is not easy to see why there was a struggle unless it was for the indirect rewards to be gleaned. We might be talking about the 'back hander' for getting a hired pool table into the centre. There may be the chance to 'pocket' the money paid by friends for using the centre laundry while the staff are out. Most negotiations between families seem to be fronted by women, though I now think that menfolk, husbands and brothers are obvious in the wings. I am sure in certain settings they are part of the strength weighed in negotiations. Careful work is done to save 'face' and to keep aggression verbal and vocal. Very seldom do families resort to fighting.

The attitude of the families to each other affects the child. I recall a child being sent home from a club because she was too young. She had been 'grassed on' by the boy next door. The mother's complaint was not that the child had been taken home, but that those running the club had taken the word of someone of another religion. Sectarianism is alive in more places than Northern Ireland.

Children experience family as more than what goes on in their home. Community work recognises the child as part of a wider family spread across a number of households. It is part of a family engaged in various exchanges with other families.

Growing up – the value of local responses

The child growing up in a poor area has to make the move from child culture to the adult culture. Schools provide much social learning as well as academic learning. However, in the school there are few useful adult models. Teachers, like community workers, are often helpful middle class people who do not provide models relevant to the child's background. The school 'dinner ladies' may be from the same class background, though many secondary schools have very wide catchment areas serving a large number of communities. Children's clubs, youth clubs, community centres that have come out of the action of local people, and are run by them, provide more by way of social learning than is provided by 'dinner ladies'. The models these people give are set in the place where the learning can be used and thus have more immediate impact.

Models of behaviour are also given by adults as they play their part in the community. When adults form a local housing action group or they campaign for a pedestrian crossing, children are present. The adults act to bring about change, but the children observe how this is done. They may even take part, by helping to colour posters, for example.

The local response to community issues, pressures and needs have an impact on the values, morals and images available to the child. This material is ready to be used later on in their lives when it may be used to create more abstract concepts.

The involvement of local people in local issues helps the transmission of culture from one generation to another. It also helps the social learning of the child. Community development can help sustain this.

Community development – a method of child care

So far this chapter has outlined the questions posed by social work. We have talked about:

> the child and its culture;
> the family in estate communities;
> the value of local responses.

I would like to look more specifically at what community development does as child care. Looking back on what has been discussed so far, I would point out three key issues which address the care and nurture of children in poor communities:

> 1) the socialisation of the child
> 2) the environment of the child
> 3) opportunities for the child.

1) The socialisation of the child

We have described the process of community development as one that helps local people engage in issues central to them. The adults engaged in this process offer useful role models and also offer insight into the social interactions on a housing estate. By being part of these events the child learns rules, norms, and local public attitudes. These things are learned 'on site' or in the actual context in which they will be used. The children can test the adult models they observe and get a sense of how appropriate they are to the setting.

The socialisation is not about being absorbed into a kind of local status quo. The child learns ways of dealing with change, as well as ways in which adults seek to promote change.

When I worked in Birmingham a community arts group started roping off and digging up a children's play area. The children themselves decided that some action should be taken over this, so they organised a protest march, making their own banners, etc. The working class parents weren't at all surprised by the children's action; they saw it as the way things had to happen. However, some parents were incensed that the middle class arts group took no action about some of the swear words on the banners. I suggest that this is an example of a pattern of socialisation at work in working class communities in which there is a strong local protocol. Community work aids this social education and has an important part to play in the growing up of children. It complements other kinds of social education found in schools and other institutional settings.

2) The environment of the child

The process of community development is one in which people get together around those issues that affect them. Very often pressures are caused by factors beyond the control of the local people, leading to the formation of associations of tenants, or residents, or streets, to translate those feelings of pressure to the sources of power. Workers support, aid and inform groups of local people in this. They help people develop stratagems and tactics to address the real issues that affect them, as far as that is practicable. A successful outcome often results in improvements to the area in which children grow up.

In the area in which I have been working, the local authority was undertaking a programme of modernisation of council houses. One road had somehow got missed out of the programme with the result that people's baths were effectively in their kitchen. Residents were particularly concerned about the effects of these conditions on their children's health. The local people set up a campaign to lobby the local authority; part of the campaign, for example, was to have photographs taken of people leaning out of their bath to remove the saucepan from the stove. The protest led to the local people negotiating with the local authority, as a result of which there were improved conditions. This improvement is expected to benefit the children.

3) Opportunities for the child

Even for quite small sums of money, those who make grants

require certain assurances. They need to know that the grant is applied to the purpose for which it was given. They need to keep in touch with those receiving the money to get an account of how it is spent.

In another area in which I have worked a group of parents became concerned about their children having nothing to do in the long school holidays. They were anxious that the children's boredom might lead them to get into trouble or to wander to unsafe places – eg, railway lines – in their search for adventure. By forming themselves into a voluntary group the parents were able to bid for funds from the local authority. This opened up a whole range of opportunities for the children on that particular estate.

Poor areas may not have strong organisations of local people. This is one reason community development workers are engaged in the first place. In *The Making of Community Work*,[5] David Thomas refers to this aspect of community work as part of the 'distributive function of the Welfare State'. The presence of the community worker implies the presence of their employing agency, or some umbrella organisation to which local people can relate. This in turn offers a range of resources – for example, holiday schemes, training and learning programmes, play equipment not normally available. All these resources mean opportunities otherwise denied to the child.

Conclusion

The reader may not feel that there is a proven case from these illustrations. However, there is enough evidence available to warrant a proper examination of the evidence that community development contributes to:

  1) the socialisation of the child
  2) improving of the environment
  3) more opportunities for the child.

Community development methods take into account the communities in which children grow, not only in the sense of being neighbourhood based, but in the sense that they see a child as a growing person not a static entity. The background factors discussed are the child's own culture, the ways in which families operate in communities, and the adult models offered to children. These factors are often treated as marginal issues by modern bureaucratic welfare agencies. One way of making these concerns less marginal is for agencies to give more attention to the community development aspects, and to make such methods more central to their service.

References

[1] Holman R. *Resourceful Friends: Skills in Community Social Work.* London: The Children's Society, 1983.

[2] Opie I and Opie P. *The Lore and Language of School Children.* London: Granada Publishing, 1977.

[3] Rutter M and Madge N. *Cycles of Disadvantage.* London: Heinemann, 1976.

[4] Abrahams P. Social networks, social change and neighbourhood. *Social Services,* February 1980.

[5] Thomas D N. *The Making of Community Work.* London: George Allen and Unwin, 1983.

Joe Hasler has been involved in community work for 15 years in a variety of settings – Birmingham, Essex, and Liverpool. Since writing this chapter he has moved on to Bristol to lead one of The Children's Society's new diocesan community work teams.

TRAVELLING HOPEFULLY – A PROJECT'S JOURNEY

Celia Burn

This chapter traces the involvement of The Children's Society on the Derbyshire Hill estate in St Helens between 1979 and 1986. It shows how the approach and design of the project changed as the work developed in consultation with local people. Many different agencies and individuals were involved in the development of the project; this account does not attempt to cover the viewpoints of all the participants. Rather it aims to show how one large national voluntary child care agency attempted to respond to the needs being expressed by a community. This is just a part of the full story of the Derbyshire Hill Family and Community Centre.

St Helens is an old Lancashire town which is now (reluctantly) a part of Merseyside. The town has had three main industries – mining, chemicals and glass making; this last dominates the town and the Pilkington family are still influential. The recession hit St Helens later than many other areas in the North West but the early 1980s saw whole factories and industries closing down and larger firms making drastic cuts in their workforce. Although it is less than 20 miles from both Liverpool and Manchester it has very little to do with either of these great conurbations and retains a strong identity of its own.

Derbyshire Hill does not fulfil the image its name conjures up – of green fields and a gently rolling landscape -- far from it. Derbyshire Hill – or Durby Hill as it is known locally – is on the edge of St Helens in the shadow of the power station and the pit, with spoil tips and slag heaps providing the only hills. Derbyshire Hill has three distinct areas. Firstly, there are the 'old avenues' made up of pre-war council housing which has had some renovation and refurbishment but needs more. Secondly, there are the 'new avenues' of post-war council houses and finally, 'cement city' which describes some of the early system-built houses provided by the National Coal Board for its employees. Much of the housing is in need of repair and Derbyshire Hill is considered one of the 'hard-to-let' estates of the town. It is a well established area, however, and people identify with it strongly.

The total population of Derbyshire Hill is around 9,000 and growing; the local schools are all full. Families are relatively large, those with four or more children being quite common. The stability of the area results in strong family links, with parents, grandparents, brothers and sisters all living in the neighbourhood. Changes are taking place, however, and the latest census figures show that the number of one parent families in the area has doubled in the past ten years and is twice the average for St Helens as a whole. Unemployment is high, approaching 25 per cent at the time of the 1981 census but now nearer 50 per cent. The closure of Bold colliery in 1985 added to the stress on some families who were still suffering from the effects of the preceding miners' strike. In 1983 a student on placement at the social services office on the estate conducted a survey of referrals to that office over nine months. Over 65 per cent of referrals related to financial, fuel and housing problems; the financial problems forming a major part, indicating the extent of poverty in the area.

One section of the community most aware of the stresses being placed on families was the congregation of St Philip's Church. The vicar, Ted Longman, became acutely aware of these problems on one particular weekend when church members were forced to take a family into their care when pressures became so great. This led him to approach The Children's Society with a request for a social worker to be attached to the church to assist the vicar and other members of the congregation in their work with families on the estate. In April 1980, six months after the original approach, The Children's Society appointed Bob Toan as a neighbourhood social worker in the area. Bob Toan and his family moved into the area; this was an important factor in the development of trusting relationships with local people and he received a great deal of advice and support from the church.

Initially, Bob Toan worked with individuals and families identified by the church and by social services. As he came to know people better he became more involved with some of the community activities. St Philip's Church was extending its involvement into the community and as a member of the church Bob was able to contribute a social work perspective. The vicar passed on any specific social or family problems which he encountered to Bob. Bob worked closely with social services, particularly the community development officer, and with the local authority to set up a single homeless accommodation project for young people (SHAP). As well as having a close working relationship with the church and the local social services office (he carried a caseload), Bob was involved in a number of community activities and groups, in particular, the Residents' Association and Derbyshire Hill Play Action Committee. This contact made him aware of the need for a community facility which would provide not only a meeting place but also some of the practical resources needed. Apart from a few pubs and the Bold Miners' Welfare Club, the area had few social or recreational facilities. There was a local authority youth club situated at one end of the estate but the only other meeting place had been the church, which was used not only for worship but also for a playgroup, old-time dancing, brass band practice, jumble sales, an after-school club and much more. This presented practical problems for both the church and the groups.

The first stage – buying the garage

When, in 1981, an old coach garage next to the church came on to the market, this seemed too good an opportunity to miss! It was not an inspiring building – not much more than a large square brick box – but it had potential and it was ideally situated near the centre of the area, next door to the church, the post office and the bus terminus.

Two surveys were carried out. The first, a structural survey of the building, discovered that a large tree at one corner of the garage was undermining the foundations, and the tree could not be removed as there was a conservation order on it. It seemed to be a major setback until, in a summer gale, the tree was blown down and the scheme was under way again.

A second survey was carried out to discover what local people felt was most needed in the area and how they felt a project should be managed. The survey showed that a meeting place, a launderette and sports facilities were thought to be most needed. The survey also showed that people did not want the centre to be run by the council, or for that matter by any one major organisation. Instead they felt that if the centre was to be a true community centre then the community should have some say in how it should be run. There were differences of opinion about how this could be achieved. Some felt that the guiding hand of the professional would always be needed; others felt that in principle the community should run the centre itself but they were not sure how this would work in practice.

A steering group was set up to guide the project through its early stages. This group was made up of representatives of the various bodies involved and a number of local residents. The group soon split into two, with one group (made up of professionals) discussing the financing of the project and the details of how the work was going to be undertaken and the second group (comprising local residents with some of the professionals) working out what would be best for the area. There was some overlap between the two groups.

As the plans became more ambitious, so the cost of the project went up from £80,000 to £180,000. The professional group set themselves the task of raising this amount and by the summer of 1982 the full amount had been promised. The first £25,000 was used to purchase the garage and secure its future as a family and community centre. The venture seemed risky at this stage and the only local organisation in a position to take such a risk was the church; the building was therefore purchased by the Diocese of Liverpool and the parish of St Philip's. It was understood that once a community association was formed it would lease the building from the Diocese. To meet the needs expressed in the survey, the building would include a sports hall, two meeting rooms, a coffee bar, a shop, a launderette and community office.

Alongside the fundraising for the building, discussions were taking place about how the centre would be run. Who would be in charge? How would the running costs (heating, lighting, etc) be met? How could the community retain its voice? These discussions led to the formation of a constituted body which would allow the interests and views of all parties to be expressed.

Reconciling differences – the formation of the community association

Early in 1982, Bob Toan announced that he would be leaving The Children's Society and the area later in the year to train for ordination. This led The Children's Society to re-assess its involvement in and commitment to the estate. Discussions took place between the Assistant Regional Director for the region and the Social Work Director of The Children's Society to determine the Society's future involvement in Derbyshire Hill. It was agreed that 'more of the same' would not be appropriate and that a new partnership needed to be formed, not just with the church but with the community as well through the community association.

In a memo to the Social Work Director at this time the region's Assistant Regional Director described this as "a new departure for the Society which hitherto had agreements with local authorities and not participatory agreements with communities: their residents and church". The Social Work Director pursued the concept of partnership in his reply: "Partnership with local groups would usually be with the aim of the local group taking over and not merely as a matter of principle". An agreement was reached with the community association that The Children's Society would provide a centre manager and, when the centre was complete, a centre worker. These workers would be responsible for day-to-day decision-making within the centre while remaining employees of The Children's Society. It was expected that after five years the community association would be in a position to run the centre itself without the support of the Society, financial or otherwise. There was no clear outline of how this would be achieved but there was an awareness that the next worker appointed to the project would need skills other than those of a social worker. A new job description was drawn up which changed the emphasis from working with the church to working with the community association and furthermore stated that the worker's job would be to train the members of the local management committee to run the centre themselves. It was recognised that the new job would therefore need a person with skills and experience in community work rather than social work. There was always a concern that The Children's Society's values and its primary interest in children and families should not be lost, but the presence of the Society worker on the management committee of the association was considered sufficient to guard these interests.

Bob Toan left in August 1982 and I took up the new post in November. I had previously been working as a community development officer with a new town development corporation and had a background in community education. Although I had had experience of setting up a community association elsewhere, the complex nature of the project at Derbyshire Hill presented a new challenge. The first meeting I attended just before starting work for The Children's Society was the inaugural meeting of the Derbyshire Hill Community Association.

For some months before the inaugural meeting, a small group, with the assistance of a solicitor who gave his services free of charge, had been drawing up the constitution of the association. This constitution allowed for permanent representation on the association's management committee from The Children's Society, Merseyside Improved Houses (a housing trust with property in the area who were able to provide technical assistance to the project), the Diocese of Liverpool, St Helens Metropolitan Borough Council and the Parish of St Philip's. The bulk of the membership, however, was to be made up of representatives of groups operating in the area and individuals living in the area. The management committee was elected at that inaugural meeting and there was a strong sense that the committee was going to be a powerful body and that representation on that committee was important.

At the first management meeting of the new community association the members suddenly realised that along with power went responsibility – in this case the responsibility for spending £180,000 and creating a new community centre. At that point some local people attempted to hand power back to three of the professionals on the committee, (The Children's Society worker, the local authority's community development officer and the vicar) by suggesting that the three of us should meet regularly with the architect and others involved with building the centre and should report back to the committee every six months.

This suggestion was strongly resisted – particularly by the professionals concerned – and instead the committee decided to try to break down the operation into identifiable tasks for which small groups could be made responsible. Several groups were set up immediately: one to deal with the building work; another group to explore the financial aspects; a third group to discuss the functioning of the centre. This method of working enabled local people to increase their knowledge and skills and so become more confident in speaking at management committee meetings; it has become a standard way of working for the community association, particularly when any new or difficult issue arises.

One of the principles established at that first meeting was that it was a new venture for us all, community representatives and professionals alike, and that although we would always try to make the right decision, mistakes would be made. Over a year later one member of the committee told me that by being given 'permission' to make mistakes she had felt freed to try things out and act in a way that had not been possible before.

As no-one had had experience of chairing meetings, it was decided that for the first year chairing the committee should rotate. From this emerged a chairperson who successfully guided the association through its early years.

The Children's Society representative on the management committee was the community worker/centre manager; I was also elected secretary to the management committee. This meant that as well as having to meet the Society's requirements I was also answerable to the community association and carried out the decisions of the committee. This could have caused conflict, but both organisations recognised the benefits of the partnership and no conflicts arose. For me, this partnership solved one of the major dilemmas of community work – accountability. The community association was able to have direct control over those tasks that were undertaken on behalf of the association eg, handling correspondence, preparing papers for the committee meetings, taking minutes, carrying out specific tasks agreed by the committee. The other element of my work

– the Society's involvement as an agency in the development process – was worked out and negotiated with the association. There was an understanding that I was there for a limited time only and that ultimately much of my work would become their responsibility. There were times when this was uncomfortable for me. As the community association increased in confidence, however, their understanding of the role of the Society developed and they too became aware of the constraints.

The building progresses – planning for the future

Work on the conversion of the bus garage into a family and community centre began in January 1983. There were setbacks, particularly in relation to costs. A promise of free labour never materialised and the labour costs incurred immediately put the project over budget; furthermore, some of the figures given for the heating system and the roof were grossly underestimated. Another major fundraising attempt was launched and eventually the total amount of £250,000 was raised. Some difficult decisions had to be made at this time; the committee was dependent on advice that it received from professional experts, and decisions were made even more difficult as the experts constantly disagreed amongst themselves.

In March 1983, however, we learnt that the community association had been awarded an Urban Aid grant of just over £10,000 a year for five years towards running costs (but excluding any salary). This gave the association control over the running costs, but it raised important questions about the relationship between The Children's Society and the community association. As the Society had committed funds for five years only, what would happen at the end of that period? How would the Society be able to manage a building that it did not own? How could the Society's worker maintain her position on the management committee when holding such an important post?

These dilemmas were discussed both within The Children's Society and with the community association. These discussions raised questions about the Society's stated aims and the community association's role. Was the Society's aim to set up and run the centre efficiently or was it to work with the community association so that it could do this itself? If the community association was really committed to running its own centre then it would have to take responsibility for staffing as well. This was not an easy decision for the association, but it was agreed that this step should be taken. The Urban Aid grant was re-negotiated with the local authority and the Department of Environment to include £5,000 towards the salary of a centre co-ordinator, with the association agreeing to make up the rest of the salary. This also meant that The Children's Society had to consider how the money it had budgeted for salaries could best be re-allocated to ensure the success of the project.

The Society agreed to use the money to pay some of the running costs, to pay cleaners (until the association was able to take this on itself) and to provide training opportunities for local people in management and community work. It was also agreed that the Society's worker would have no responsibility for the building but would act as a development worker with the association as well as being a full member of the management committee.

Working together

The success of the project was dependent on how the partnership between the Society and community worked out in practice. For example, it would be important to achieve equality on the management committee with the views of local people given equal consideration to those of the professionals. This is not always easy to achieve. The professionals in such a group have advantages of training and education, and experience in talking in meetings and putting across ideas. Local people may not have the experience or the confidence to challenge the views of the professionals or to understand the jargon used. The difficulties of trying to achieve equality were experienced in other areas. Before equality can be achieved, the inequalities have to be acknowledged – professional workers had to be aware that as well as their professional skills they also brought with them advantages resulting from differences in class and education, leading to inequalities of power, status, knowledge and access to information. Members of the community needed to feel confident that their knowledge of the area and of people's needs and their commitment was recognised and valued. As knowledge was shared and learning took place on both sides, so the relationship became more equal and power began to shift from the professionals to the community.

My main responsibility was to ensure that the members of the association recognised the skills and knowledge that they already possessed and also to provide opportunities for them to learn new skills. To achieve this I resolved to do nothing on my own. It was particularly important that representatives of the community attended any negotiations with the council or with funding bodies and expressed the needs and aspirations of the community. Such meetings were carefully planned to ensure that the case was well put.

Underlying all my work was the basic belief that everyone has the potential to grow and to develop new skills. These skills may not necessarily be acquired through formal training programmes (although this may be appropriate in some cases, eg, in training as a playgroup leader) but rather through a process of action and reflection – planning an activity, carrying it out and then reflecting on what went right or wrong, using that information on the next occasion so that the same mistakes are not made again.

To ensure that the project progressed, however, certain practical tasks were allocated specifically to me. I attempted to work as openly as possible so that people could see what I was doing and also learn from my mistakes. Over a period of time local people took on more and more responsibilities and my role became more that of a consultant.

The centre opens

The centre co-ordinator was appointed in March 1984, and shortly afterwards the office was opened. Before the centre opened, the committee had to tackle problems with the floor in the main hall; shortage of funds meant that the members had to lay the floor themselves.

The centre soon became a focus for community activity. It offered practical services like the launderette and the public telephone which brought people into the centre who had not previously been involved. This created new tensions. Some members of the committee who had seen the centre through all its difficult times resented newcomers getting involved when all the hard work was over and the fun was just beginning. This is a common experience in community work – that those who have the vision to bring an ambitious plan to fruition then get pushed to one side by those who want to get on with the action. At Derbyshire Hill these dangers were recognised and discussed, leading the management committee to emphasise the value of everyone's contribution in the development and future of the centre.

The main principles of the association laid down and embodied in the constitution were never forgotten. It has always been seen as particularly important to retain openness and acceptance, to share the association's values and principles with new members of the management committee and in this way develop a centre ethos.

Four years on

At the time of writing the Derbyshire Hill Community Association has been in existence for four years. The centre is flourishing. It is open from 9.00am – 10.00pm (sometimes longer) seven days a week, and offers a wide range of activities to all members of the community. There is a youth club and playgroup for mentally handicapped children run by parents; a playgroup and an after school club; a summer playscheme run by local volunteers (in 1987 they took a group of children away on holiday); a number of sports activities – the karate group has over a hundred members aged from 4 to 54 – a keep fit group. One of the features of the centre is the number of activities in which parents and children can join together. During the day the centre is used mostly by families with young children. A number of adult education courses have been held in the centre and there is close liaison with the local community schools. The centre is used by pensioners and by a group of unemployed people. A welfare rights advice service operates from the centre and members of the residents' association are always on hand to answer any housing queries. The coffee bar is open most of the day and serves a range of snacks.

A simple description of activities does not really convey the atmosphere of co-operation and commitment in the centre. There are many examples of co-operative working: when the playgroup needed a new playhouse but could not afford to buy one, volunteers from the camera club obtained some wood and made one; every year, the parents and friends of mentally handicapped children group organise a door-to-door collection and most of the volunteers for that are drawn from the centre. The management committee is able to respond quickly to issues that arise and the centre is very often the first place people come to if they have a problem.

As well as the centre co-ordinator, the association now employs five MSC workers who form an administrative support unit for the management committee. This has released management committee members from some of the more mundane tasks in the centre to undertake more exciting developmental work. Funds are now being raised to develop the land around the centre into a five-a-side football pitch and recreation area. Members of the association are at present exploring the possibility of purchasing their own transport to undertake outings for the summer holidays and trips to the lights at Blackpool. The annual revenue budget, including the centre co-ordinator's salary, is approximately £25,000. The grant from Urban Aid is still £10,000 which means that the association has to raise £15,000 a year just to break even, without taking into account money needed for new projects. Much of this income is generated by the centre itself: the launderette and the coffee bar make a small profit; the profit from the pay phone almost pays for the cost of office calls; a charge is made for hiring rooms, which is reasonable compared with similar centres; a small entrance charge (usually no more than 10p) is made for activities organised by the association. The association has found many other ways of both saving and making money; equipment and materials are obtained free from local firms which helps to keep costs down; services are offered that people are willing to pay for – for example, photographs of the children in the playgroups are taken at reasonable rates at the centre and commission from the photographs goes to the association. By providing services that people need at a price they can afford the association is able to use any profit to benefit the community.

Working with others

The Children's Society and St Philip's Church have been the two organisations most closely involved with the growth and development of the association and the centre. The association's relationship with the St Helens Borough Council has been more erratic. Senior officers of the authority were involved in the early days of the project and were fully informed of the plans for the centre. Officers of the authority were responsible, in conjunction with the association, for submitting the successful applications for Urban Aid. The community association recognised the need for a good working relationship with the council, not only because the Urban Aid grant was administered through them but also because of all the other services that the council could offer the association. The Derbyshire Hill Community Association was the first organisation of its kind in St Helens and the potential for community growth and development that it provided was not immediately recognised by councillors or some council officers. For the first year the authority was represented at management committee meetings by officers, in particular the Community Development Officer for the area, who was able to offer a great deal of advice and support. However, in 1984 a change in the political make-up of the council resulted in a change of policy towards voluntary organisations. Councillors became anxious that organisations which were receiving grant aid through them should be accountable to them. Councillors were nominated to sit on the management committee to provide this accountability. However, for almost two years, during the re-structuring of the local authority, no councillors attended meetings and communication with them was difficult.

When the community association applied to the council for a substantial sum of money to cover the deficit on the building work, councillors began to take the association more seriously. They attended management committee meetings and learnt at first hand about the association and the centre. Initially they appeared to see themselves as 'troubleshooters', but gradually they began to realise that the association had its own mechanisms for working out problems and that their contribution could be to provide a channel of communication between the association and the council. They also recognised and came to value the energy, time and commitment of members of the management committee.

The Children's Society was able to fulfil a bridging role between the community association and the council. Workers from the council felt able to relate to me because they saw me as a fellow professional. At times this was frustrating as I was seeking recognition for local people as equal partners. I felt, however, I could act as the 'community's professional', acting on their behalf and in consultation with them. The role can easily be abused and I referred constantly to the community to ensure that mis-representation did not occur. Local people were always involved in negotiations and discussions and now local people deal with the council direct. Professional workers from the council are also learning that they need to listen to local people in order to find out if their services are being effective.

The achievements of the community association provided a valuable model for other groups in the borough. The council now recognises that properly constituted voluntary organisations can attract money to the town that would not otherwise be available. It also realises the need to be responsive to local communities. More community development officers are being employed to support voluntary groups, and money is being put into community education projects. These developments have led to better relationships between the council and voluntary organisations throughout the town.

Looking ahead

It will be clear that my role changed considerably over the years. Initially, I was carrying out many of the centre co-ordinator's tasks. I was also concerned with managing the association's money and was directly involved with most of its business. As members of the community have taken on most of these tasks and the association has employed its own workers, my role has become increasingly that of consultant and adviser. I still carry out tasks on behalf of the association, eg, organising training opportunities for local people, but at the same time involve members of the management committee in many of the tasks that I had originally undertaken.

Within the region, The Children's Society is developing other community work projects and I find myself becoming more involved with other Children's Society work. This has resulted in a gradual withdrawal – negotiated with the management committee – from the day-to-day running of the centre.

The association has less need now for the intense involvement of The Children's Society. Good relationships have been established with local authority community and play workers, and support and resources can be obtained from them as well as from other local voluntary agencies. The Children's Society does have a long-term commitment to and relationship with the community association; it will always be able to maintain its involvement through membership of the management committee. The role of The Children's Society was described in the report to the Social Work Committee at the end of 1984;

"The role of the Society within the overall project is to provide and promote a philosophy which will determine practice and govern the behaviour and relationships of those involved, both in formal committee meetings and in informal groups; between agencies and individuals. It has been the worker's role within the project to maintain the belief that local people are able to make decisions and take action that can affect their lives, and to reflect this belief back to them. There is a delicate balance to be maintained of influencing values within the project without devaluing the local community. This requires the worker to sustain and confirm local people in their actions and their growing awareness of their power and roles".

The development of the community association in Derbyshire Hill and the Society's involvement in it may appear to have little to do with the Society's direct work with children and families. A visit to the centre, however, would soon reveal that children are the major focus of work for the association. All its work is aimed at improving conditions in the area; not just facilities but also housing, health, and education, all of which directly affect the lives of children. Individual families can receive advice to ensure that they are receiving the benefits to which they are entitled. Families are able to meet together to discuss common problems and work out solutions. The Children's Society has had a part to play in the development process and will maintain its links in the future. The decision making and control of resources, however, will be firmly in the hands of the local community.

The report of the project made to The Children's Society's Social Work Committee in 1982 aptly described what changes took place after Bob Toan's arrival:

"When the worker arrived he brought with him the more traditional forms of social work intervention; but over the years he has evolved different community-based approaches as constituting more effective methods of intervention that meet needs. ... The worker originally moved to the area wanting to 'do things to people' - so to speak - but is now increasingly aware of the necessity of being alongside people whilst they do things....

In an area which is highly stigmatised, when people are seen doing things for themselves it has great impact on those individuals and families involved and others. Being successful in organising events and schemes; making approaches to statutory agencies(like housing and social services departments) and being heard; setting up playschemes and annual fetes; all are important things that do absolute wonders for people's self esteem and feeling of self worth. The worker, by being able to affect small groups of people in this way can have a positive effect upon how they are able to cope in their own families with their lives. Because people are more able in a sense to help themselves, it also releases them to be able to look outward and give support and assistance to those who are in difficulty."

Celia Burn was an infant teacher in Oxford for four years before moving to Liverpool in 1973 to set up a community education project working with parents and pre-school children. She worked at the Open University developing parent education materials and at Warrington New Town as a community worker before joining The Children's Society in the project at Derbyshire Hill. Celia is now Assistant Regional Director for the Society's North West Region and maintains an interest in Derbyshire Hill.

ISSUES FOR COMMUNITY PROJECTS DEVELOPING LOCAL INVOLVEMENT

Rosie Edwards

In this contribution I will explore the process of local involvement in one particular neighbourhood project. I will investigate whether contact with individual users seeking help or advice inhibits local involvement or is one of the preconditions for local involvement. I will also consider how we can best promote local involvement in the future.

What is local involvement?

The process of local involvement is crucial to community work. Community work sets out to develop the skills, knowledge and abilities of individuals and groups in a given community in order to increase the influence and power they can exert over their lives. Community work places emphasis on the poor, the powerless, those lacking in resources. If people are to gain resources, influence or power, they must first become involved in their community. In isolation each person's resources and opportunities will remain limited, but if a person begins to work with others in the community, he or she can derive strength and confidence to tackle issues and increase access to power and resources, which may ultimately improve their quality of life.

In a community project staff seek to involve local people in the life of the community. A project does not consist solely of a building or even a range of activities. Indeed many community projects are sustained by a community worker with neither premises nor facilities at his or her disposal. The

Millmead Project, on which this article is based, has a small building, a team of staff and a small budget.

The Millmead Project team attempts to use the building and its resources as a pattern for community involvement. By involving local families in the project and increasing their influence over the direction of its development the team hopes to demonstrate that local involvement can result in genuine benefits for the community[1].

Why is there a project on the Millmead Estate?

In its centenary year (1981) The Children's Society proposed to open 12 family centres; the Millmead Project was one of these. The Society was closing East Court Children's Home in Ramsgate. Kent County Council was also closing many of their own children's homes at this time in favour of fostering and attempting to keep children at home in the community. Discussions between Kent Social Services and the Society showed a wish to maintain a Society presence in Thanet. Jan Phelan's research for The Children's Society[2] indicated two areas of Thanet with high incidences of children going into care or receiving custodial sentences – Newington in Ramsgate and Millmead in Margate.

The Millmead Estate is part of the Northdown Park Ward. Some 500 council dwellings (houses and a high rise block of flats) were built in the late 1960s and then in the 1970s 1000 private houses were built and subsequently sold to the district council, and the council built a further 100 flats. The issues Jan Phelan identified in 1980 remain in 1986. Unemployment for Thanet as a whole had risen from 9.4 per cent to 20.7 per cent (Job Centre statistics). On Millmead one in three adults of working age were registered unemployed in December 1986. Although 25.2 per cent of the population of Thanet as a whole was of pensionable age in the 1981 census, Millmead Estate has very few retired people; young families predominate. Millmead had the highest number of juveniles known to social services going to borstal or to detention centre (1976-1986) for Kent. Thanet overall had the highest proportion of single parent families in Kent (135 for every 1000 families), and the highest percentage of children taking free school meals (25 per cent). More recent studies by the University of Kent at Canterbury and Thanet District Council not only confirm these trends but emphasise Millmead's position as a high need area within Thanet, which itself is a high need area of the south east.

The estate itself has few facilities. The telephone box on the new estate is invariably vandalised, the one on the edge of the estate is frequently out of order. There is one shop on the estate (small general shop), a small parade of shops a mile away, and the main shopping areas in Margate (two miles) or Cliftonville (one mile). The church, school and park are on the northern edge of the estate (on the smart side of the road). The estate is bounded to the south by the railway line, public open space (the old tip) and the road from Margate (which peters out just past the turn off from the estate).

The dwellings are two- and three-bedroomed terraced houses and a series of one- and two-bedroomed flats with gas central heating (using air vents rather than radiators). Many of the homes suffer from condensation (or damp, depending on your viewpoint). There is vandalism on the estate, but it does not live up to its reputation of a 'pigsty' (a newspaper quote by a district councillor in 1985). Packs of unattended dogs are an intermittent problem, however, intimidating residents, causing a nuisance and polluting the grass verges.

What sort of project is the Millmead Project?

Millmead Neighbourhood Centre is based in a three-bedroomed council house in the middle of the newer part of Millmead Estate. When the project opened in 1981 residents were encouraged to drop in for advice or to meet staff. Staff initiated several activities at the centre in response to local demand; these ranged from a boys' snooker club to adult literacy classes. Staff found it hard to sustain local involvement in the activities or in the project. A new staff team arrived in the spring and summer of 1984. We told local people who came to the centre that whilst the staff and the building were resources for them to use, the staff would not run services or activities. We would, however, assist local people in running services or activities and also try to develop the resources available locally, in co-operation with residents.

When we explain the components of the project, it is often quite difficult for people to understand the distinctions we make.

We seek to present the project as a resource to local people; that includes staff, the building and all elements of the work. We seek to work in partnership with, and with the participation of, local people. A resource can be moulded, used, developed by all parties involved. A service, on the other hand, is provided by one group of people for another group of people. It has a more limited opportunity for involvement, being based on the assumption that once a need is established a response is provided. It may be that within the Millmead framework facilities are developed but the emphasis is on the residents defining not just the need, but the response too.

An information leaflet distributed to local residents in autumn, 1985 described the project thus:

> "Millmead Neighbourhood Centre is a community
> project staffed and funded by the Church of England
> Children's Society with grant aid from Kent County
> Council. Its purpose is to work with local people to
> encourage and develop facilities, activities and
> opportunities for children and families in the Millmead
> area of Margate."

What motivates people to use the project?

The centre is used by a variety of individuals and groups: their motivation can range from anger, anxiety, loneliness or boredom to curiosity, concern or interest. The project team keeps a daily diary, analyses use of the centre and talks with users and groups about use and non-use of the centre. The groups which use the project choose to call themselves 'house groups'. These groups meet with staff every month to share news and to develop their involvement in the project. Staff and house groups try to publicise the centre and its facilities by a variety of methods, including use of leaflets, posters, newsletters, press and local radio coverage; they also make great use of word of mouth contact. From the daily diary we identified seven reasons for people using the project.

1) Telephone

The project has an office telephone and a payphone 100. Use of the telephone has always been one of the main reasons for people coming into the centre.

2) Borrowing equipment or resources

Local people can borrow anything from a hoover or lawn mower to camping equipment or the project minibus. During 1985 the team started to develop a resources room containing books and leaflets which people can borrow or use. This room also houses an electronic duplicator, a stencil cutting machine, a typewriter and simple audio visual equipment.

3) Information

People enter the project with a variety of requests for information, from children enquiring about play activities to adults finding out about bus timetables.

4) Advice

People mainly ask for advice on matters relating to welfare benefits, housing or financial problems. They do, however, also come to the centre with personal problems and issues relating to health, education and the social services department.

5) Community involvement

This category covers those who come to plan or organise activities, people who are interested in a particular idea and come for help in putting it into practice and those involved in community groups who come in for support and encouragement.

6) Liaison and organisational contact

We receive visits from social workers, health visitors, clergy and others in the caring professions or in community work. We are also in regular contact with colleagues in The Children's Society.

7) Activities

The major single reason for entering the building is to take part in an activity. A range of 16 activities for children and adults take place at Millmead Neighbourhood Centre. Details of these activities are given below.

Date	Activity	Initial Idea	Planned by	Run by
1983	Friday Club	Staff	Staff/volunteers	Staff/ volunteers
Pre-1983	Gingerbread	Local single parents	Local single parents	Local single parents
1983	Adult education	Local college of further education	College in liaison/staff	College tutors
1984	First Steps playgroup and parent support group	Parents	Parents/staff/ health visitors	Volunteers and health visitor
1984	Baby clinic	Health visitor	Health visitors	Health visitors
1984	Playaway group	Parents	Parents and staff support	Parents
1985	Tuesday Club	Staff	Staff/volunteers	Staff/volunteers
1986	Youth Evening*	Youth	Staff/youth	Staff/volunteers
1986	Arts/crafts/ drama*(teenagers)	Staff/youth	Staff/volunteers	Staff/volunteers
1985	Playscheme committee	Parents/house groups	Parents and staff support	Parents
1985	Advice service CHIP**	from CHIP	CHIP and staff support	CHIP
1985	House group meetings	Staff	Staff and house groups	Staff and house groups
1986	Community buildings group	Meeting of house group and agencies re local facilities	Local groups and staff	Committee and strong staff support
1986	Parent/toddler swimming	Parents	Parents and staff support	Parents and volunteer driver
1986	Coffee break	House groups	Individual users and staff	Small group of users (4) and staff (1)
1986	Lunch break	House groups	Individual users and staff	Small group of users and staff

*   Youth activities were a development of previous
     activities started in 1985
**   Community Health and Information Project. This does
     not include the many people who seek staff advice in the
     course of a week.

How do people become involved in a project?

As the previous section shows, many local residents use the
centre at Millmead casually – they use the telephone or
borrow equipment, they drop in for a chat or request simple
information. Staff encourage casual or informal users to
return to the centre or to bring other members of the family
to the centre. As staff learn more about users' interests or
concerns they will try to draw them into the life of the estate,
either into activities based at the neighbourhood centre, such
as playgroups, or into involvement with the community
outside the centre, such as babysitting or offering help to a
neighbour. The chart in the previous section gave details of
the development of the activities of the project. I should now
like to explore the issue of user involvement through the
development of three of those groups.

Playaway Playgroup can be traced back to August 1984. A
group of eight mothers and their toddlers had been coming to
the centre twice a week for nearly six months. Some mothers
stayed with their children but most did not and the range of
play equipment was poor. The new project leader met the
mothers to discuss what type of activities they would like for
themselves and their children. The mothers suggested that
there should be a playgroup for older children (3-5 years), and
a playgroup for the under 3s with the chance for mothers to
meet as a group with a health visitor while the children were
playing.

Two mothers, who were already involved in the summer
playscheme at the centre, volunteered to run the playgroup
for older chldren. For a year they ran the group and also
studied and completed the assessment on the Open University
pre-school playgroups pack. At the end of that year they
announced their resignation for personal reasons. Meetings
were held with the mothers and four mothers decided to take

responsibility for the continuation of the playgroup. All four women started coming to the centre through contact with their health visitor, who was running a mothers' group attached to the under 3s' playgroup (one of the four had attended the earlier mums and toddlers meeting in 1984). Two of these mothers undertook to train at the local technical college and become the playgroup supervisors. One year later they continue to run the playgroup, which is a valuable local facility. The playgroup is able to operate at low cost because it has support from the project and because the supervisors only claim expenses.

Community education groups are one way of stimulating local people's skills and self confidence. Over the past two years, Millmead's neighbourhood worker has publicised and set up six different community education groups. One example was a 'fix it yourself' group. The original idea for this group was discussed with centre users, and six sessions were planned, teaching basic skills such as mending a tap, putting up shelves, fitting a pane of glass. The sessions were publicised through the local adult education service, through local leaflets and by word of mouth. All those who attended had seen the local leaflets but decided to attend after conversations with staff at the centre or with other users. More came through the local adult education service.

After the six planned sessions, the group continued to meet for a further two terms and called their meetings 'skill swap'. This was an opportunity to further their new skills, learn more skills and involve a wider group of people. Through word of mouth contact the group doubled in size although week to week attendance depended on individuals' particular interests. Although the group dissolved over the summer holidays, all but one of the core group went on to other activities and have remained involved in the life of the estate.

Dane Valley Playscheme was set up in spring 1985. A number of mothers sent children to activities at the centre, but were not involved themselves. The neighbourhood worker made a point of seeing these parents and talking to them about local play facilities. A group of them met for coffee several times and then decided to form a committee to run a summer playscheme with the help of the neighbourhood worker. Dane Valley Playscheme catered successfully for over

100 local children with help from other centre users, several
more parents, volunteers from the church and local youth
centre and centre staff.

Early in 1986 they decided to enlarge their committee.
They leafleted the estate, arranged publicity in the local press
and contacted other house groups at the neighbourhood
centre. People responded to the leaflet and the committee
doubled in size. One or two of the new members were already
involved in local activities, some were casual users of the
neighbourhood centre, and two were new completely. The
new committee managed to plan, finance and run a creditable
fortnight of summer play activities, including three long
distance outings.

Most of the people in these three studies have continued to
use the project in a variety of ways. Three have become
volunteer drivers, six have learnt how to use the duplicator,
all have used the information in the resources room and ten
have used the advice service.

These examples have shown how individual people can
become involved in the project through group activities. It is
more difficult, however, to establish a pattern of involvement
for casual users of the project. Most casual users eventually
seek advice. This can range from advice on DHSS single
payments to a request for advice on problems with children.

Jack, for example, would pass the time of day with staff in
the street long before he came to use the telephone. It took
months before he asked for help with a welfare rights
problem. Once that problem had been resolved, however, he
began to talk about other worries. He also got involved in
helping with some of the centre's activities for children.

Jill, on the other hand, has used the centre for over three
years and still only comes in to use the telephone. Her
children have never regularly attended activities. The main
difference between Jill and Jack seems to be that Jill has a
supportive family in Margate, while Jack's family do not live
in the south east and he is fairly isolated. It is also culturally
more difficult for a male single parent to be accepted on the
estate.

It seems therefore that local people become involved in the
centre through local contacts and activities. Publicity and
accurate word of mouth messages stimulate their

involvement. It also seems more likely for them to get involved if the project, or a part of it, meets a need such as friendship.

The chart on page 34-5 gives details of user and staff involvement in the current regular activities based at the neighbourhood centre. The initial idea for 10 of the 17 activities came from local people, four were staff ideas and three came from local agencies. The three ideas from agencies were for services which local people requested and support. All the activities, apart from the services, were planned by a combination of people, with the after-school and youth activities having had the most limited local involvement in planning. The degree of involvement in planning is reflected in the actual running of activities – the more involvement staff have had in planning an activity, the more likely they are to retain substantial influence or control in the day-to-day running.

One of the most encouraging features of the analysis is that the most recent activities have all been instigated by local people at the house group meetings who are also involved in the activities themselves.

When I joined the project in 1984 I set out to develop a co-operative framework for the planning, reviewing and appraisal of the project. This was intended to involve everyone who had a stake in the project: staff, Children's Society, funders and local users. In 1985, the project team started a process of quarterly reviews and forward planning. These linked with quarterly meetings between the Project Leader, the Assistant Regional Director of The Children's Society and the local social services manager.

In the spring of 1986, the house groups decided that they would like to link with this process. The house group meetings are proving a valuable forum in involving users in planning and development, not only of new activities but also of the shaping of the project.

In practice it has been hard to ensure that all the meetings tied in together. We will need to allow more time in future to have more thorough discussions. All those involved, however, in particular the house groups, have said that they want to continue the system. An important principle of local involvement has been established in giving local people access

not only to the day-to-day running of the project, but also to
its framework.

Why do people stay involved in the project?

I have already observed that once people took an active part
in the project they began to use it in a variety of ways. Once
people take the first step, they gain access to a network which
can widen their circle of contacts, present them with new
ways of tackling problems and give them support.

Anne, for example, was weighed down by several problems
and first came to the centre for advice. Over a period of three
or four months some of her problems were resolved and she
began to offer her help to the centre. Both she and her
children got involved in activities at the centre. A year later
she has acquired a network on the estate which can support
her and her family and in the process ease her problems still
further. Although the nature of Anne's involvement with the
project has altered, it continues to give her benefits.

The dilemma

Community work focuses on building groups and networks to
promote long term solutions to people's powerlessness.
One-to-one work separates people and seeks individual
answers; furthermore, it can be very time consuming in a
setting where pressure is exerted by both funders and users to
deal with increasing numbers of people.

Problems suffered by many and tackled on a self help basis
are harder to ignore and stand a better chance of being
solved. However, when a community project is based in a
neighbourhood centre, residents also expect staff to come up
with an answer to any problem particularly if the centre is
virtually the only local facility. This creates a dilemma for
community workers.

Perhaps we confuse people by running a building in the
first place. No matter how hard we try to involve house
groups, residents and volunteers in the running of the
neighbourhood centre, it is still viewed as belonging to the

staff (or even to The Children's Society). We increase their confusion by providing the very services which we claim will encourage their involvement.

If residents first come to our centre to use a telephone or an advice service, it is likely to be hard to persuade them of the benefits of community involvement with its commitment and effort. On the other hand, as I have described, access to resources within a project can help to boost people's confidence and encourage them to become part of networks which will help them in their everyday life.

If one-to-one work is an essential element of community involvement, there are also other elements: the full range of publicity – oral, written and visual – and the input of staff and house groups. The neighbourhood worker has always attempted to reach users and non-users using contacts, word of mouth and publicity. She has also used the development of the house group meetings as a means of improving information exchange and sharing.

All project staff experience a tension between the four aspects of the project's work:

Activities   the support and development of key activities

Resources   a general responsibility which sustains the project and sometimes leads to new developments

Individuals   dealing both with individual users and members of groups with individual needs

Alliances   making links between different levels and elements within both project and estate. For example, house group meetings and the community centre steering group, where the former is part of the project but the latter part of the life of the estate.

As the activities develop, so use of the centre increases, expectations rise and space decreases. If people utilise its resources the project has more demands made on it and new developments can sometimes be started without adequate

planning or resources. Furthermore, when staff are under
pressure they tend to avoid dealing with complex personal
problems such as family relationships and mental health
breakdown. This could ultimately have an adverse effect on
the involvement of the very people we are supposed to be
working with. Alliances which are so vital in the long term
might be the first to be affected.

If we are to sustain local involvement in our projects it is
vital to retain a balance of the four elements of activities,
resources, individuals and alliances. I can see three main ways
in which project staff might achieve this:

1)   *We could put pressure on other agencies to co-operate with
    us or to provide direct services which would ease our load
    and resource the estate.*

We have some direct services at present such as an advice
service and an informal baby clinic. The advice service
sometimes makes work rather than relieving it. People call
when problems present, not just when the service is on hand.
The project staff then either take on the problem themselves
or become the messengers and risk giving a protracted and
unsatisfactory service. The health visitors run a good,
friendly, informal baby clinic. Ideally they could extend the
work by selling baby foods and developing the health
education aspect of their work.

Project staff have in the past sought an input from social
workers and adult education workers and are currently in
contact with community nurses. Each service seems to be
under pressure, however, and only a minority are prepared to
make the time to work with us whether in one-to-one work,
group work or staff development.

2)   *We can try to develop local alternatives to services or
    facilities we either choose not to provide or are unable to
    provide.*

For over a year we have considered training local volunteers
through Gingerbread to develop a supplementary advice
service. We still have not found time to develop this scheme.

On the other hand, we are gradually developing a family
support network using volunteers and local families. Members
of existing house groups suggested a family 'Coffee Break' and

lunch club and our new family support worker has involved local people in setting up and running these schemes which form a basis for families to meet each other. A new part-time post was crucial to this scheme.

3) We could develop alternative models for community projects.

The term 'family centre' has been used even within The Children's Society to cover a whole range of community provision from preventive to enabling and empowering work. Nevertheless, the majority of family centres contain the same ingredients: a deprived area; a building in or very close to that area; a project leader and staff; a budget with provision for salaries, premises and vehicles; funding from The Children's Society, a local authority or possibly a local church.

It seems ironic that the more ingredients a project possesses, the higher the demands made on it and the more expectations are raised by all parties. The project then has great difficulty in satisfying these demands. Some projects tackle the problem by focusing on a particular issue or age group. In practice this is very difficult if a project has set out to be community based and to involve the local community.

One or two projects have placed their emphasis on staff as their main resource. This can be very draining for staff but it can also be liberating, allowing staff to take a clear community development approach and avoiding any confusion about their role.

One of the attractions of a community development approach to community projects is that it at once introduces the notion of involvement. If we attempt to involve all the interested parties in the research and planning of a project, then we can avoid some of the pitfalls of an imposed solution such as conflicting values and expectations. This preparation then becomes a model for the running of a project. If each of the stakeholders in a project accept the notion of partnership, then it should be possible to develop a consistent policy of local involvement.

References

1 Some examples of this method of work are described in
Community and Education by R W J Keeble, published by
the National Youth Bureau 1981. See especially chapters 4
and 5.

2 See in particular *Family Centres – a study* by Jan Phelan
and *Family Centres* by Joe Hasler, both published by The
Children's Society.

*Rosie Edwards has been involved in community work in both
statutory organisations and the voluntary sector since 1972.
She is currently project leader of the Millmead Family Centre.*

MALTBY FAMILY CENTRE AND ROTHERHAM UNDER 5s – A HAPPY FAMILY OR A STORMY MARRIAGE?

Liam Condron

The idea

Maltby Family Centre (known as Prospect House) is a Children's Society community project in South Yorkshire. Maltby, a mining village of 18,000 people, lies about seven miles outside the town of Rotherham. Rotherham Borough is a large industrial area with a population of around 250,000. Industry has traditionally centred on coal and steel.

The economic decline in these areas has led to a rise in the rate of unemployment to 20 per cent. The 1981 census showed that under 5s represented 7.3 per cent of the population, as compared with a national average of 6 per cent. Local authority provision for under 5s, on the other hand, is considerably below average; up to the end of 1986 Rotherham was spending less than any other metropolitan borough on this age group. The social services department does not, at the time of writing, provide day care for this age group, though there is some part-time nursery education for children from the age of 3. The borough boasts no community work posts, and even in the voluntary sector there has been little community activity, particularly in the area of child welfare. In 1979/80 The Children's Society opened a family centre in Maltby which had, as one objective, support for groups in the community working with under 5s.

MALTBY FAMILY CENTRE AND ROTHERHAM UNDER 5s –
A HAPPY FAMILY OR A STORMY MARRIAGE?

In a 1980 survey of the Society's family centres the Maltby project registered its main activities as: an advice service open to all the community, a playgroup offering 48 places to local children, and a mothers and toddlers group run entirely by volunteers. By 1984 the advice service was preparing to move into new premises as Maltby Advice Centre. Activities with children had expanded to include: a thriving toy library serving a number of venues in Maltby; and playschemes involving 50 or more children every day of the week during school holidays and half terms. The Worzel Gummidge Club was a fixed group of about a dozen children from 6 – 11 years old referred by schools and concentrating on developing their social skills. Finally, a group of young unemployed volunteers from 16 to 25 years of age was using the family centre to congregate, to some extent as a base for social activities and principally to help with the maintenance of the centre and to make and fix things for the groups with whom we had contact.

The aims of the project at this time were: to give greater control to people; to develop their confidence and abilities; to make agencies more responsive to people's needs and to foster a spirit of self help.

The family centre had always offered support to groups in the community that worked with under 5s. In 1980 a group of local professionals concerned with development of under 5s work in Maltby began to meet at Prospect House. They drafted a proposal for future work which included a family support scheme and under 5s resource centre for Maltby. When the government announced funding for under 5s work (the Department of Health and Social Security Under 5s Initiative) the group, grasping the opportunity for greater resources, extended the proposal to include the whole borough of Rotherham and Prospect House applied for funding. In October 1983 some funding was approved. The number of staff in the project doubled overnight and the family centre's work with under 5s took on a completely new level of priority.

The purpose of this chapter is to give a flavour of the relationship between the under 5s project and the family centre; to look at the factors that determined differences between the under 5s project and the centre in approaches to and directions of the work; to look at the ways in which the philosophy of the under 5s affected that of the family centre or vice versa.

The experience

The under 5s team, comprising three project workers plus clerical staff, was based at Prospect House and was under the leadership of the project leader. The overall philosophy of the project rested on the belief that: the environment in which parents with children live can be improved; a wider spectrum of choice should exist for parents seeking help or support; and these things can be achieved through consultation with agencies that work in the community and with the community itself. The under 5s team set out to inspire and facilitate the process. The means it was to use were: information; education; campaigning; and support.

Information/education
The team used knowledge as its principal tool in motivating parents to take the initiative in child welfare. The staff aimed to increase the information available to parents on facilities that already existed and on how other facilities could be developed. A central resource room set up in Prospect House was the focus of this information service in the sense that it was a collecting point for a wide range of material on all aspects of work with children under 5.

Parents tended not to use this drop-in facility, however, so the team decided to take the information out to the community. The mobile resource, generally associated with a large yellow van called the 'yellow bug', was a representative collection of displays, leaflets and handbooks from the central resource room. This material was to be taken around to playgroups, nurseries, health centres, schools, toddler groups, libraries, supermarkets and anywhere that parents with under 5s might be found. Apart from using the 'yellow bug' the project also undertook education – both formally in workshops and on courses, and informally in group meetings of parents and indeed professionals. Subjects tackled included child care, handicap and how to set up a group. It is particularly in this setting that individuals and small groups have been motivated into action, either to provide services or to seek provision from the local authority.

Campaigning
It is notoriously difficult to educate the 'educated'. However, by using displays and events and – more importantly – by motivating parents and supporting them in their own efforts to press for change, the under 5s team aimed at increasing the awareness of professionals and policy makers of the need for improved child care provision around the borough. Particularly successful were the support for groups tackling deficiencies in nursery provision, and public meetings to press for change on a variety of issues of concern to families with young children.

Support
The under 5s team recognised the futility of simply preaching the cause of child welfare and retreating to an ivory tower. They aimed to offer: demonstration, guidance, support and encouragement.

The family centre had established a toy library, which formed the basis of the Rotherham Toy Library Group. The under 5s team gave support to the group, encouraging the establishment of ten more toy libraries, some of which used Maltby as a model. The under 5s team developed a contact with the cultural centre in Rotherham and was able to encourage a number of activities for under 5s within the Asian community. Finally, much time was invested in supporting groups of parents with particular concerns such as those with hyperactive children and with twins. The aim here was to build and nourish the groups and to help them discover ways to meet their own particular needs.

On 21 and 22 June 1986, Rotherham held its grand annual tattoo. For the first time the tattoo included a contribution from the under 5s team and the groups they were supporting; it was billed as the 'Rotherham Under 5s Facts and Fun Event'. In a large marquee, standing amidst a number of smaller tents and booths, a variety of groups set up stalls and displays exhibiting their work and talking about the concerns of families with young children. Half of the area under the marquee was dedicated purely to play, a major theme in the work of the under 5s project.

Based on a similar event which took place in London, the Facts and Fun Event was intended to be the triumphant finish to the under 5s team's work and a boost to the relatively new umbrella group – Rotherham Under Fives Together, which it was hoped would carry forward the work of the team. The actual end of the under 5s project was scheduled for September 1986.

Meanwhile in Prospect House

As stated in the introduction, in addition to setting up the under 5s team, Prospect House was expanding its own work. Over the two years since then the project leader had been increasingly involved in management and development issues. The project was attempting to respond to The Children's Society's enthusiasm for local participation and control and was developing a new relationship with the playgroup, mothers and toddlers and other groups using the premises. In its bid to respect the needs and desires of the community the project began to involve itself to an even greater degree in talking to professionals and the local authority.

The declaration of a General Improvement Area in Maltby (a government scheme which offered support to the community to improve the environment) gave the project the chance to be involved with community action. We also formed an association with the newly opened Maltby Action Centre for young unemployed people and more recently with the Maltby Employment Project. This association led to greater involvement with local people, community groups and the council.

The project's traditional involvement with play developed along the same lines with the formation of a Community Play Association. Playschemes run by the project have made forays into the community and are becoming the responsibility of the association. As the project has moved more into development and away from service provision, certain pieces of work have been allowed to run down – eg, the unemployed volunteers' group, and others – like the 8-11 year old referral group (the Worzel Gummidge club) – have been dropped.

One area of service provision that has continued to be supported is the advice centre. The project's response to this support has been to increasingly leave decisions in the hands of volunteers, and the eventual aim is that the centre will be run almost entirely by committee while continuing to be resourced by The Children's Society.

The relationship

There is no useful metaphor for the relationship between Prospect House and the under 5s team. It has been difficult to see the under 5s team as part of Prospect House. It has an individual identity, its own philosophy, its own team meetings and can generally stand alone as a separate project. In this respect the relationship has been simply an acquaintance. At the same time the under 5s workers were managed by the project leader, from whom personal and professional support was also required. In this way the under 5s team was part of the Society's almost familial structure. In both professional and structural issues, there was a deeper level of sharing, sometimes joyful, often painful. The relationship, in this respect, was something like a turbulent marriage.

When we have worked together on material for the Society's Appeals Division, for example, or shared information on our particular areas of work, or helped on a more practical level by appearing at each other's events, lending support and sharing the work load, we have felt very positive about our relationship and consider these occasions as times of growth. We have not always felt as positive about our relationship in the more contentious areas of team meetings and on management issues, but even where tensions have existed between the two teams, they have not always been negative. Occasionally, differences between us caused us each to examine our values, challenge inconsistencies in practice and forge a new philosophy.

Apart from structural differences between the projects, such as length of funding and the ratio of part-time to full-time workers, there were also differences in the approaches to work or frames of reference. The most obvious is, of course, in respect of the particular area of work. While Prospect House has been involved in a wide variety of activities including under 5s work, the under 5s team has concentrated principally on families with children under 5. It may or may not be a structural concern that all the under 5s workers were women and have been sensitive to the women's issues inseparable from the under 5s work, while the Prospect House staff have been predominantly male. Prospect House has always had commitments throughout the borough but it is first and foremost a local project working with and for the community of Maltby. The under 5s project had a much wider brief – to improve facilities for under 5s throughout the Borough of Rotherham. Some activities in Prospect House are run by groups of volunteers for the community, whereas in the main the groups the under 5s project have had contact with are self-help groups. Prospect House has always had a substantial amount of face-to-face or direct work with individuals. The under 5s team has only rarely been involved in this sort of work, having concentrated rather on developing and supporting groups.

Some of these differences have caused, as has been stated, destructive conflicts and some constructive. The under 5s team's concentration on a particular issue and on tackling the shortcomings in provision has challenged Prospect House to justify the need for a broader base of work in a single community. In the same way the local nature of Prospect House's work has challenged the under 5s team to justify spreading itself more thinly throughout the borough. The less constructive result of these differences has been some degree of isolation. At its height, this isolation exhibited itself in a five month sojourn by the under 5s project into the middle of Rotherham. There was even a suggestion at this time that it should be constituted as a project separate from Prospect House. Even this conflict, however, had its positive side. When the 'two projects' did a major evaluation of their work in 1985 the differences were absorbed and justified and the two projects agreed to a single philosophy. The philosophy addresses the issues of working with people rather than simply for them and tackling the root causes of disadvantage. While it stresses the importance of Prospect House's local nature it acknowledges the participatory style of the under 5s project.

Where are they now?

The under 5s project did not in fact finish in September 1986 but was given a reprieve of six months. Winding down the project would inevitably be difficult and it is to be hoped that the extra time will allow loose ends to be tied up to the satisfaction of the project workers. Among those loose ends will be the need to ensure that groups that have relied on support are able to stand on their own. The team also felt that it wanted to have some tangible evidence of three years' work. The team has produced a booklet containing information about facilities for under 5s in Rotheram and a video about the under 5s project and the groups it has worked with. A further document is to be produced, tracing the developments of the project and its effect on facilities for children under 5 in the Rotherham Borough.

Finally, it will be necessary to ensure that somebody monitors those facilities that do exist, develops them and continues to press for improvements in local authority provision. It was intended that the previously mentioned umbrella group, Rotherham Under Fives Together would take on this role. The group is as yet only loosely knit, but it is still planned that they will take forward provision for under 5s in Rotherham.

As previously stated, the family centre is currently contracting, or rather consolidating, its work. The project is now looking far more to developing resources within the community or, where no such resources exist, to pressing the local authority to provide them.

Work with young people will be increasingly tackled through the Maltby Play Association. The advice service will be run by local people and volunteers. An under 5s worker will remain to develop the Rotherham Under Fives Together group and develop facilities in Maltby by providing resources, support and motivation.

So what?

So what effect has the under 5s team had on the development of work at Prospect House? To say that Prospect House's position in the community, its concerns or its approach to work would have been the same regardless of the under 5s team would be to ignore the efforts of four highly competent people over a period of three years. Equally, to suggest that the position Prospect House now holds bears no relation to the plans it made three years ago, or that the experience of the under 5s project was vastly divergent from the plans made for it, is also unacceptable.

It is probably true that the philosophy of Prospect House stems more from the development of its thinking on broader issues in the local community and the enthusiasms that are emerging in The Children's Society than it does to the particular approach or style of the under 5s team. This may be due in part to the isolation created by the under 5s project's concentration on its own issues, and its base in the borough rather than in the community of which Prospect House is a part. Another reason may simply be that while in number the staff of the under 5s team is comparable in size to the staff of Prospect House, under 5s work nevertheless, represents only one of many areas of concern to the wider project. At the same time, however, as Prospect House prepares to take on the commitment to develop Rotherham Under Fives Together and address the issues of under 5s in Maltby it must be recognised that the awareness and enthusiasm of the whole project for under 5s work has grown immeasurably.

The practical effects of the under 5s experience, apart from the indirect benefits of increased funding, must surely concern the management of the project. The result of the inclusion of a short-term funded project into a long-term one is difficult to forecast. The management of an infusion of part-time workers is not an easy task. Supporting a team working throughout the borough on a particular issue from the experience of a team working locally on a variety of issues is likely to be quite demanding. Taken altogether those factors represent a cost to the project not just materially but also in terms of morale. The task of any manager or project is to plan on the basis of a balance between cost and benefit.

The final question must be whether the experience of the under 5s project has had any lasting effect on future planning. In the project evaluation of 1985 the management and staff involved in Prospect House made a firm commitment to keep alive the enthusiasms of the Rotherham Under 5s. That commitment remains: in the person of the new under 5s worker; in the commitment to the development of Rotherham Under Fives Together; in the encouragement of the people of Maltby to seek out adequate provision for their under 5s and to participate in making decisions about how resources can be used to the community's best advantage.

Liam Condron is involved in several aspects of community development in Rotherham. He is chair of the Rotherham branch of Child Poverty Action Group and the Rotherham Welfare Rights Training Group. His role at Maltby Family Centre has been on the welfare rights side of the project.

PART 2 – PLANNING AND EVALUATING COMMUNITY PROJECTS

The articles in this section address critical issues which need to underpin neighbourhood projects. The concepts and language of planning and evaluation can seem alien to the feelings which surround the day-to-day life of neighbourhood projects, but unless they are present, those projects will at best have a limited existence and at worst come seriously to grief.

A paradoxical lesson for neighbourhood work is that, precisely because it encourages openness and participation, the need for staff to structure their work carefully and on a team basis is overwhelming. The nature of the work will place unexpected demands on the practitioner, and it is easy for him or her to become caught up in a succession of activities which, when examined closely, fail to cohere.

The guide to planning given by Peter Wiggin provides a spine or central core of working principles for projects. This planning process is directed at the setting-up phase of community projects, but inevitably this will determine the subsequent direction of projects. He writes from the viewpoint of a regional manager, and as a result addresses matters such as negotiation with the local authority and funding. One has a sense of being on the boundary between the organisation's concerns and the involvement of local people in the project. This is as it should be – the manager or planner with his or her feet firmly on the ground.

On the other hand, Derek Akker's arguments for treating assessment of a project as an ongoing process derive from the perspective of a project leader, the person who has responsibility for implementing the planning. Inevitably there will be tension between a concern to monitor and reflect upon a project's activities and the wish to fuel the activities themselves. There is a parallel between the need to set out the arguments for ongoing assessment and the need to make the case for an inter-agency strategy within a community setting. The potential benefits of both are not immediately obvious. The inter-agency work analysed by Ruth Hall provides answers to such doubts. She places three examples of inter-agency projects with which The Children's Society has been involved within a theoretical framework. This use of theory helps the reader to identify critical issues in a difficult, complex and relatively underdeveloped area of practice – at least in the UK. At the end of her paper Ruth Hall discusses some ideas which could help The Children's Society take its inter-agency approach further.

The last contribution in Part 2 also makes strong connections between the experience of setting up a project and theory, in this case the published material on evaluation. Neil Proctor and Jenny Sayer's use of this material gives the business of evaluation and the need for it to form an integral part of a community work project clear relevance to practice. British community work is littered with examples of how good intentions in this area have failed to be carried through. The model offered by the authors can be picked up by practitioners and adapted to their circumstances. The issue of evaluation of community projects is unlikely to go away.

Thus the following articles address some of the key elements of the infrastructure required by community work practice: planning, evaluation and links with other agencies. These are the organisational components which lie behind the open, face-to-face engagement of a project with local people. The evidence is sufficient for us to know that, while these components may lack immediacy, they remain essential buttresses for effective, sustained practice.

COMMUNITY PROJECTS –
A GUIDE TO PLANNING

Peter Wiggin

Introduction

This paper offers a guide to planning community projects. I have tried to approach this task in a practical way and so share some of the lessons that I have learnt with others involved in developing similar work.

I write from my particular organisational perspective as an assistant regional director responsible for development and management of work within one of the six regions of The Children's Society. I would not wish to suggest that the issues I have discussed provide a comprehensive framework for planning, nor that the way I undertake my particular task necessarily reflects the way my colleagues in the Society operate.

As a means of illustration I will refer to the Beckhill Family Centre in Leeds. This is a recent project which has benefited most from the experiences that I and my colleagues have had over the years, and the planning for this project follows most closely the systematic planning process that is outlined in this paper.

I will be making many assumptions during the course of this paper and do not wish to offer lengthy definitions of the terms that I use. Broadly speaking, the guide will be of most benefit to people planning projects which are sometimes referred to as family centres or community projects and follow a community development approach.

I also need to acknowledge the fact that The Children's Society operates within a clearly defined context directed towards the needs of children. While this focus does not lead to separation from the families and the community of which they are a part, it does mean the Society would not consider work where either direct or indirect benefit to children is not the prime consideration. In spite of this focus I hope that the planning outline considered in this paper will also be relevant to the development of community projects that may have an emphasis on different groups.

Preparation stage

The period of preparation for a project can be a long one; my experience is that short cuts at this stage can have disastrous consequences. The importance of thoroughly identifying need and establishing clear reasons for starting work in the most appropriate form based on a sound value framework cannot be overstressed.

Evidence of need

Evidence of social need can be established in many different ways. Sometimes our organisation is approached by a local authority with a specific request for us to meet a clear social need that they have identified. In this case it is important for the organisation to undertake its own enquiries. In one case a local authority approached the Society to set up a day care service. Closer investigation by the Society suggested that the needs of families and young children would be better met by a completely different approach. This example stresses the danger of defining needs in service terms. In other cases our own enquiries may identify a particular community with evidence of the background indicators of social concern; such a community is often found in an inner city area or on a large estate in or around a major town.

In the case of Beckhill in Leeds, our initial brief had been agreed with the local authority. This was to set up some form of project which would focus on an area of high disadvantage in the city and would complement the work of existing agencies. After much investigation of well known areas of concern we concentrated our attention on three separate districts; each had clear indicators of social disadvantage with a high proportion of families with young and teenage children.

In one of these districts, arguably one of the most deprived in the city, several welfare initiatives were already being developed in the community and we therefore decided against continuing our enquiries in this area. This example serves to illustrate the obvious importance of balancing clear evidence of need with existing resources.

Evidence for helpful co-operation and partnership with residents and agencies

It is also important to investigate existing and potential co-operation and partnership with both established agencies and residents' organisations. In the case of the statutory agencies, there may be important funding implications in co-operation; without an early commitment from those agencies to contribute direct funding or to support funding applications, there may be little point in continuing to make plans. Equally important is the relationship with various voluntary organisations and residents' groups. Much goodwill and trust has to be earned and may take a long time to develop, but if the potential for such a relationship is minimal, the effort is not likely to be worthwhile.

In the case of Leeds, a good working relationship with the local authority departments, and particularly the social services department seemed possible as previous work by the Society had been undertaken in the city. Initially no statutory funding was available, but the authority expressed a readiness to explore future possibilities. In one of the districts that we investigated local political tensions could have made planning a fraught and uncertain task, and this certainly influenced our eventual decision to develop our project elsewhere.

Acknowledgement of the value of a community-orientated approach

The sort of community project which I consider has the greatest potential for benefiting residents is either neighbourhood based, or set within a local and clearly defined community. It is also important that there is scope for building relationships with all the various groups in the community. A community-orientated approach by its very nature seeks to be inclusive and non-discriminatory; the presence of many groups with a narrow interest would clearly present difficulties to such an approach. Once again, in another district under consideration in Leeds, some groups were undertaking successful work within the minority sections of the community, but there were also considerable tensions between some of these groups which would have made it difficult for us to operate in the way that we preferred.

Clarify the value base and approach
I would argue that the success of a community project depends a great deal upon the shared philosophy and value base of both the host organisation and the individual members of staff responsible for undertaking the work. Where a gulf exists between the organisation and the individual workers, then problems are likely to develop. Equally, the staff members require a sound understanding among themselves if they are going to work together successfully.

The Children's Society has a clear basis for common agreement insofar as it is a Christian based organisation with a clear statement of philosophy. However, differences of opinion and approach can exist within this framework and detailed team work has to be undertaken to establish a project philosophy which will guide the development of work and reflect the values and attitudes of the staff.

At Beckhill, participation is a central theme and one which I consider crucial to the development of community work. Participation implies that people are treated positively as unique individuals with a contribution to make, rather than negatively as groups who may share a common debilitating characteristic. It also acknowledges the right of people to be fully involved in identifying the issues and concerns that affect them; by the same token it acknowledges their right to be fully involved in meeting the needs that they have identified.

Participation also encourages those people who may have only a limited contribution to make to share their talents with others. This gives benefit to both giver and receiver, and as such is an essential means of promoting human capabilities as well as feelings of worth and dignity. It is also a means of countering the helplessness often deeply felt by individuals and communities in the face of circumstances which may appear out of their control. In this respect participation is a means of increasing power.

At Beckhill we also refute the notion of 'prevention', together with the use of the term itself, which to us perpetuates a negative concept. Instead we prefer to use the term 'promotion' which more closely represents work which is based on positive beliefs and results in constructive benefits.

In planning our new work in Leeds we were fortunate in having an existing group of one full-time and three part-time workers who previously worked from a Society family centre in the city which had been forced to close. These workers formed the team for the new project. There was a common understanding not only between the team members but also between them and me. However, we spent a considerable amount of time exploring and developing a common basis for working together within this new development. We particularly wished to stress the values of 'participation' and 'promotion'. This meant that we would seek to operate in a way which encouraged the involvement of local residents, with the inevitable conclusion that increasing elements of power and control would be transferred from the workers to the local residents as the work developed. This philosophy would also lead the staff group to operate as 'enablers' rather than mere providers of a service. An early recognition of a clear value base underpinning new work was crucial at this stage of preparation and had wide ranging implications for future planning.

Outline plan
When the initial planning work has been completed it is useful to summarise the outline proposals in a plan that will guide future development and be of use in negotiation. This plan may only be brief; however, it should indicate clearly the basic aim and the intended objectives for the proposed work and should describe the value base that will guide the approach. It should also include proposals for funding, staffing, accommodation and management, together with timing targets for implementation.

Following the initial planning work in Leeds, we finally decided to set up a community-based project within the Meanwood district, to the north of the city.

Negotiation stage

Consultation and agreement

This is a most crucial stage. The outline plan described in the previous section can provide the vehicle for receiving approval from the host agency and can also form the contract that may be agreed with a partnership organisation in appropriate cases. In the case of Beckhill the outline report was agreed by the regional management team of The Children's Society before being forwarded to the Society's headquarters for approval by the Director and Social Work Committee. The importance of agreement being reached at different levels within any organisation cannot be stressed too highly. Even if there is no organisational procedure for reaching such agreement with either the host or a partnership agency, the effort spent seeking a common understanding at this stage can sometimes prevent serious difficulties occurring later on. Where shared resources are being considered, the need for explicit agreement is even more vital. It may well be that further planning cannot proceed until funding resources have been both confirmed and made available.

There was no financial constraint at this stage at Beckhill, as initial resources were being provided exclusively by The Children's Society. However, there was joint commitment to one important resource – namely, property. I will examine this issue in more detail later in this paper; here I will say only that lengthy negotiations took place to secure suitable council premises, without which it would not have been possible to proceed.

It is always difficult to establish how much consultation and negotiation should take place with local residents early in a project's development. The arguments in favour of early consultation are very strong, particularly for a project which will be based on the principle of community participation. However, my own experiences make me suggest a note of caution; expectations can be raised too early which are then dashed with quite harmful consequences if the planned development has no chance of being realised.

During the preparation and negotiation stages for Beckhill, we consulted with relevant professional staff from agencies and key local people whom we considered could fairly represent the feelings of residents; we did stress that it was possible that nothing would result from our enquiries. However, local people were to become fully involved with planning at the next stage and we deliberately made no firm decisions about methodology and practice until this could take place.

It is also important to involve voluntary groups and elected council representatives in discussions during planning and negotiation. There was little organised voluntary activity on the estate we were investigating, with the exception of the local churches. However, three ward councillors whose areas covered the council estate were involved; the active support of one of these councillors proved decisive in reversing an early decision by the Housing Officer who turned down our application for council accommodation.

Establish long-term plan

During the planning and negotiation, it is necessary to establish and consider the implications of a long-term plan. In community development work this should include consideration of the issue of local control. The Children's Society has produced a report on 'Community Involvement and Local Control' based on the findings of a working party which looked into all the practice and organisational implications of the agency's desire for greater participation by local people in its own projects. The Society concluded that whilst complete local control may only be attainable in a small number of its community projects, the principle of moving in this direction has implications for all work. Such matters have to be considered at the earliest stage of development of a project.

Sadly, organisational requirements such as funding often have undue influence over the nature and length of community initiatives in the voluntary sector. It can be tempting to accept short-term funding and to plan around this without fully anticipating the problems that are likely to result when funding ceases. I would argue strongly for greater realism in setting up new work. However secure the basis of a project, uncertainty over funding severely limits an ability to plan ahead with confidence. The resulting uncertainties for both staff and local people can severely undermine the aims of the work being undertaken, and the consequences of having to close prematurely can be quite disastrous.

At Beckhill there was a long-term plan to withdraw some staff involvement. This reflected a strong desire to encourage participation and discourage dependence on the project workers. At the same time, the recognition that withdrawal may only be partial, acknowledged the likelihood of a continuing need for some enabling and service support for any subsequent residents' group taking over a greater degree of control. A research study undertaken by Leeds University has now been established at Beckhill to measure this movement and to help us plan for the future, and share with others the lessons that we have learnt.

As a large national organisation with a more secure funding basis, The Children's Society is not totally dependent on local authority financial support. I recognise that this gives us a secure base, which may not be shared by smaller organisations. My only plea for all concerned in long-term planning is to maintain realism.

Formation stage

Appointment of project leader and staff
Staff would not normally be appointed until the negotiation stage has been completed successfully. I would consider the appointment of the project leader to be the first step to take; the qualities required in this appointment should be fairly clear if the stages described have been worked through.

If there is a strong emphasis on local participation in the project, then local opinion should be represented. At Beckhill this was not possible; as previously stated an existing staff team had been appointed to the project.

Induction and support of the project leader must be thought out. The degree of support required should not be underestimated, particularly where work is being undertaken in an intense and perhaps depressing environment, perhaps initially in isolation from other staff. Where additional staff are to be employed then it seems sensible for the project leader to be settled in and to have a good idea of the qualities required to complement the staff group before appointing.

Detailed survey, analysis and plan preparation
The best way of becoming familiar with an area is to get out

and about and meet people. While a framework will have been provided for development in the outline plan, more detailed planning will need to be undertaken if future work is to be soundly based. Also, the process of undertaking a detailed survey is arguably as valuable as the end result in providing opportunities for outreach to local residents and agencies.

A certain amount of information about need will have been accumulated at an earlier stage, but I would stress the advantages of a detailed investigation within more clearly defined neighbourhood limits, together with an analysis of the information gathered. There is much valuable information available about undertaking a social survey and The Children's Society has produced a helpful guide.[1]

The detailed survey report that we completed for Beckhill included sections on: the geographical and historical background to the area; industry and employment; population; public amenities; and existing statutory provision. The results of this survey helped us narrow the focus for intended activity on the Beckhill estate within the Meanwood district.

The Beckhill estate was built about 13 years ago and appears to be quite an attractive estate, offering a range of housing units which includes flats, maisonettes and semi-detached houses, all of which are council owned. According to the 1981 census the population of the estate was 1,742 which comprised some 715 households. Compared with the three other neighbourhoods in Meanwood, Beckhill had the highest proportion of children under 4 years of age and between the ages of 0-15 years, as well as the highest proportion of single parent families. The estate had an almost total lack of any form of community provision, and was described by the local social services community worker for Meanwood as being on a 'downward spiral'. It is obviously essential to learn about the feelings of local residents, and some sort of interview process also offers a valuable means of introducing staff and the broad outline of the project to the local residents.

The Beckhill staff visited other community projects which had undertaken similar forms of investigation before drawing up the social survey. The aim was to make the survey simple, brief and as unintimidating as possible. A sample of 60 houses was chosen at random from the electoral register, with an adjustment to include a higher proportion of houses on the road in which the project was to be based. A letter of introduction was sent a few days before the visit alerting people to the fact that someone would call at a specified time. If people were out when the interviewer called, only two further visits would be made.

Some further changes were made to the sample, so that we could include a high proportion of families with young children, and after seven weeks the exercise was complete. A total of 50 interviews were conducted, 38 with families with children of school age or below, 3 with families without children and 9 with people who were elderly.

The results of the social survey confirmed assumptions about the estate. The families interviewed included 65 children under 5 (50 per cent of all children).

Residents also expressed feelings of isolation and depression, complaining that there was no opportunity to make contact with others and almost no facilities on the estate. In particular, there was concern that there were no facilities for young children apart from a playbus which visited on only three half days a week and could only cater for a small group of children over the age of 3 years. The small play areas on the estate were described as unimaginative, unsuitable and unsafe.

Proposals for the project to develop resources and facilities for young children received the most enthusiastic responses. Some 72 per cent of those interviewed were families who had children of playscheme age, and 44 per cent were interested in having a playscheme on the estate; similar interest was shown in a mother and toddler group being set up.

The survey provided useful information but also gave most valuable contact with residents, and interest in us quickly spread. After the survey had been completed, final project proposals were drawn up.

Project base
It is easy to become tempted to look for a project base too early. Inappropriate premises can wrongly determine how a community project operates.

At Beckhill we were tempted to consider buying shop premises that came on the market early in our investigations in the Meanwood district. Fortunately we decided against proceeding with negotiations and withdrew our offer, despite losing some credibility as the owner was a prominent person in the local community.

Had we continued with these plans we would have been forced to operate from a base on the edge of Beckhill within two distinct communities which we now know to be very different from each other. Our developing philosophy and aims would have been compromised by the location, not least because it would have been difficult to transfer control of such a property to local residents. In the event, we decided to limit our search for premises within two central roads on the Beckhill estate. The premises would necessarily be council owned and we considered this to be desirable for two reasons:

a) it would facilitate a move if necessary, and encourage greater user control;

b) it would more readily identify us with the needs and aspirations of local residents and so, we hoped, provide a better basis for outreach.

During this period of negotiation we were fortunate in having a temporary base in the centre of Leeds. However, early discussions with the Leeds Housing Department were difficult and our application for council premises was turned down.

Only after a great deal of negotiation and the valuable co-operation of a local ward councillor was our appeal eventually upheld by the housing committee.

The size of property chosen as a project base must also be considered carefully. We decided that too large a building could hamper our plans for partial withdrawal and also affect the extent to which we worked in the community. In the event, we were allocated a three-room maisonette, just where we wanted to be and with some adaptation we had two comfortably sized rooms for use by groups as well as a kitchen and small office.

Project evaluation

While planning new work takes a lot of time and effort, it is also important to monitor and evaluate the work and thereby be open to making changes and improvements in line with the aims and objectives of the project.

Both evaluation and, to a lesser extent, research are important features of The Children's Society's family centres. Most projects include evaluation as part of the annual procedures to make plans and prepare budgets. At Beckhill the staff have also identified their clear need for space and time as a group. On Fridays the project is now closed to local residents and set aside for staff to review practice and for other organisational and administrative business. Needless to say, this decision was not taken lightly, but it does acknowledge the particular needs of the staff team.

The involvement of local residents in the evaluation, plan making and research work is something to which we are committed, and this is reflected in the way we operate. We are equally aware of the need to be self critical and to promote greater involvement, with the desire of achieving user participation.

Conclusion

Planning the development of a new project is a time consuming and demanding activity. It can be tempting to seek short cuts. However, if you do so, much may be sacrificed at a later stage. I would like to stress again the value of the planning work, which can often be as valuable as the outcome itself. Once again, opportunities lost at this stage often cannot be regained because of the pressures that build up after a project has opened (for a summary of the planning process see appendix).

At the time of writing, Beckhill Family Centre had just had its first birthday which more or less coincided with the arrival of the hundredth local resident to join in one of the many activities which take place. To begin with, staff took a more directive role, but now the users' meeting has greater control over the activities which develop. The holiday playscheme, given priority by local residents in the community survey, was one of the first events to develop from the family centre using the premises of a local school. This established contact with a lot of parents and more than 60 young children, who regularly attend holiday playschemes, ably run by increasingly confident local residents and supported by staff. These are now a permanent and popular feature on the estate.

As a staff group, we have learned a lot during the course of the year. We sometimes wonder if we were right in our desire for smaller premises which are greatly stretched by a whole range of activities which operate there. However, the hospitable and friendly atmosphere which has been created within the building is perhaps one of its most acknowledged achievements. Every credit must be given to the local people who have responded to the desire for their increasing participation and are showing growing concern for their neighbours. This is encouraging on an estate where isolation and lack of involvement were such common features.

Reference

[1]   Stone W. *Identifying Social Need.* London: The Children's Society, 1980.

Peter Wiggin began his working life as a town planner. He spent eight years in local authority social work, first as a child care officer then in various jobs in social services. He has worked in The Children's Society for a similar period, gaining wide experience in project development. He is currently Assistant Regional Director in the Society's North East Region.

APPENDIX – PLANNING A COMMUNITY PROJECT

A systematic process guide for the planning of community projects.

Preparation stage

Is there clear evidence of need?
Initial regional and local comparative analysis. Relate this to existing resources.

Is there evidence for co-operation and partnership with residents and agencies?
Stress the importance of a potentially good working relationship with relevant agencies (particularly with partnership projects)and local residents/groups.

Have you acknowledged the value of a community-orientated approach?
Define terms; consider benefits of neighbourhood approach, but stress potential difficulties.

Have you clarified the value base and approach?

IF 'YES' PROCEED TO NEXT STAGE

OUTLINE PLANNING EXERCISE

This summarises information obtained, establishing the outline aims and objectives and the value base for the project and providing an overall outline for the negotiation stage.

Negotiation stage

Have you undertaken consultation and agreement?
with local representatives and agencies and within own

organisation. Stress the importance of being explicit and achieving agreement through the organisations.

Have you established a long-term plan?
Need for forward planning and consideration to be given to degree of local control to aim for.

Do you have funding?

IF 'YES' PROCEED TO NEXT STAGE

Formation stage (the first six months)

Appoint project leader and staff
Issues of appointment process, induction and support must be cleared.

Prepare a detailed survey, analysis and plan
Pay special attention to residents' view, framework and approach.

Project base
Consider appropriateness,size, cost,etc.

Project evaluation
Importance of evaluation linked to plans. Must also give workers time and space.

ASSESSMENT AS A PROCESS

Derek Akker

This chapter looks at assessment in the context of a small neighbourhood project in Rochdale. The project focused on children and their families in relationship to the neighbourhood in which they live.

The development of many community projects follows a pattern of: negotiation, research, action, reflection. The term 'assessment' is often used to describe the fact-finding exercise included in the research phase and the term 're-assessment' is applied to the period of reflection. I would like to argue that assessment is a continuous process and that as such it is a tool in the development of the project. I will examine this in the context of the project in which I worked.

The first phase in the development of any neighbourhood project, the period of negotiation, is one of the most crucial. Phelan[1] has shown that negotiations begin for many reasons which include both formal requests and informal conversations. Both the funder and the agency may bring to the negotiating table their own agendas; these do not get fully aired at this stage but play a crucial part in the outcome of negotiations. The period of assessment has begun. It is during this phase that the parameters of the project's function and its relationship with the funders are established. Such parameters are governed by the expectations of the funders and the methods the agency can employ to respond to those expectations.

The product of effective negotiations is an agreement that establishes relationships and the interaction between funders and the management agents, the aims and objectives, the constituents and the duration of the project. These negotiations seldom involve those who are to implement the decisions – ie, the staff of the project. It is, therefore, imperative that those involved in negotiations should provide a sound baseline from which staff can work. This baseline should be articulated clearly, but should not be rigid. The project should be allowed scope to respond to issues that arise as the project develops.

The negotiations for this project were protracted. Discussions began in 1980, but were stopped because of financial restrictions. Had negotiations continued at this stage they would probably have led to the development of a project which provided traditional social work services. Negotiations were re-opened when Urban Aid funding became a realistic option.

The Urban Aid application defined the aims of the project as:

"to offer support services intended to create the conditions conducive to the success of the individual and family, to enhance their social functioning and self esteem, to help them to view themselves as active participants capable of change, to help them understand and use the resources available to them locally".

To attempt to achieve these aims, the project would develop a number of activities, including a mother and toddler group, a women's group, youth clubs (7-12 years), a playgroup and holiday playscheme. It would also offer supportive services – for example, welfare rights advice and counselling; opportunities for education, including Open University and health courses; and material resources. The application for Urban Aid was successful, and negotiations between the local authority and The Children's Society began in earnest. Senior staff on both sides were involved in these negotiations and a project leader was appointed who was also included in the negotiations.

The social services department was anxious to increase provision for children and families in the area. The Children's Society strongly resisted attempts to base the project on a model of service delivery, though it was accepted that there would be an element of social care. Experience has shown that it is difficult to ignore the personal issues people bring to a community project. If these problems are not addressed, they can cause confusion between problems affecting groups

WORK

and those that are personal issues unrelated purpose.

The project was aiming at 'community d looking to develop a centre for families and ch ...cn was relevant to them as a community; it was accepted that offering resources to them might form part of the work. The Society was also committed to the principle of participation. Participation within the project is a 'process where the objective is to provide opportunities for the users to participate in organising activities, taking action and moving activities and groups forward.' We believed that participation would be crucial to the development of the project, as the ability to participate is most likely to make a long-term difference to people.

Users were to be seen not as 'passive victims of society but as active participants who are potentially capable of change'. Participation would therefore be viewed as a process, of necessity open ended, which assists the users to acquire the attitudes, skills and concepts to enable them to take part in decision making.

At this stage the process of assessment moved into its second phase, into the period of research. This research set out firstly to increase the factual knowledge of the area. The aim was to investigate: the population and its composition; the type, quantity and quality of property; the available services; what employment was immediately available in the locality. In this particular project we also had access to information on the numbers and types of referral to the social services department and the load on the existing social work services.

We also contacted senior officers from various local authority departments – eg, housing, social services, planning. Contact with these departments, besides giving factual information, can give important insights into the philosophy and aims of the department and of the authority. Ward councillors also provide a means to gain further understanding of the area and how decisions are made; their insight into the political environment can be invaluable.

In addition, there is contact with local people. This contact, particularly with those engaged in community activity, can indicate the degree of cohesiveness and the nature of value systems present in the neighbourhood.

The facts gained through this sort of research form a basis from which a response is designed. The research may, however, reveal constraints that can affect the final design.

Previous attempts at participation have shown the difficulties in engaging neighbourhoods in participation. In the case of Hill Top, realistic goals were set, but the project had placed itself at the limit of the participatory process. Thus the project, while remaining in the mainstream of The Children's Society's philosophy, is in a position to facilitate change and further extend the boundaries of participatory models of work.

In exploring the limits of participation, there is also a need to be realistic as to how many local people will wish to participate in the project's development, and why. Users will participate in the life and work of the centre for a wide range of reasons – some will wish to contribute to a resource from which their neighbourhood or their own children will benefit; others may see themselves as leaders and may equate this with power; others may hope for financial gain. The question of who becomes involved and how they respond is crucial to the development of the centre.

The area in which the project was to work was agreed, and the research began. The research was based on a variety of documents – small area statistics, council minutes, back copies of local newspapers, reports and publications concerned with the estate – and on conversations and meetings with residents past and present, senior officers in the local authority housing, planning, education and social services departments.

The project was to be located on an estate, most of which was built after the second world war. The early houses, built with the assistance of prisoners of war, were completed in 1948 with further developments spanning the next fifteen years. There are currently 2,400 houses (7,000 people) on a 300 acre development of houses and low rise flats. About half of the estate (880 houses and 360 flats) have two bedrooms; a further 550 houses have three bedrooms; the remaining accommodation includes bungalows, single bedroom flats, bedsitting room accommodation, a few three-bedroomed flats and 16 four-bedroomed houses.

The socio-demographic research indicated that the estate had more than average levels of social disadvantage, when compared with the borough and with Greater Manchester. We had access to social services referral and caseload registers (not case records) which gave a clearer picture of social services involvement in the estate.

The estate was not without communal facilities. It had had a community association for 30 years, and a community centre since the early 'sixties. However, the association was encountering problems, as identified by the warden of the community centre in the early 'seventies. It had become preoccupied with activity within the centre and had thus become inward looking. It was failing to 'nurture' the community. A number of people interviewed in the course of the research spoke of the decline of the estate. Most referred to the 'seventies as the turning point, though other evidence suggests that the decline could have started in the 'sixties. In 1968 the estate made the headlines in the local press with the headline 'people are leaving Kirkholt for a decent life.'

Our research highlighted, amongst other things, apathy and indifference on the estate. To some extent the estate fits a description given by Thomas: "in varying stages of despair and disorganisation (where) people have withdrawn from communal roles and responsibilities." People had not totally withdrawn from communal roles, but the roles had become less effective, with responsibility being taken by fewer people. The community appears to have felt powerless to bring about change.

The factual and anecdotal information derived from this research was invaluable in helping project staff understand the community. This in turn enabled them to help residents themselves understand the estate more clearly.

The research also brought to light an interesting difference between this project and other family centres. Other family centres had been located in areas which were either established estates with little neighbourhood involvement or in new town developments where the neighbourhood development was in its infancy.

This estate included estate schools catering from infants up to secondary level (although the school catchment area boundaries were not co-terminous with estate boundaries) and also had a number of other resources. As has been mentioned there was a community centre, with a community warden;

this was a social centre which had a large number of activities that did not involve estate residents. The activities which were of interest to us were those which involved children. There was a playgroup, a playbus for under 5s that visited the estate twice weekly, a junior youth club, a playscheme group which organised Easter and summer playschemes, and a child health clinic which was open twice a week.

In addition to the funding of this project under the Urban Aid Programme, funding was available for a youth centre and an educational guidance centre designed to offer both formal and informal advice to parents of pre-school and school age children. The Children's Society was involved in some of the early discussions on how this new educational service would operate. The original idea was to bring parts of the education service closer to the children and their parents and to develop closer links between school and parents.

What was underestimated was the potential for apparent duplication of the work of the education centre and the family centre. This did cause problems which required some discussion between the two centres to establish co-operation. A second conflict arose after the project was set up. The housing department decided to place on the estate two community workers who would specialise in housing matters and work with tenants to create greater involvement in management and planning of the estate. This development, while having its positive side, did undermine some of the project's plans.

The work of the project could not be seen in isolation from other new developments. The task would be to see how we could co-ordinate our work on the estate and how such co-ordination would be consistent with the principles of participation.

From the information we had gathered we were able to assess the most suitable location for the proposed project. The local authority had agreed to make available two three-bedroomed houses on the hard-to-let list (thus not depriving anyone of a home).

Two properties were offered. The first was rejected on the basis of its geographical location: it was situated in a part of the area which would limit accessibility. The second property, on the other hand, was well situated and easily accessible.

A traditional view, equating assessment with the research phase, has many dangers. Firstly, the completion of a detailed assessment can be seen in itself to offer a passport to success in the creation of a neighbourhood project. Secondly, having once completed the assessment it can take on the form of a plan of action that cannot be changed. Such a plan can so dominate thoughts and actions that it can prevent staff facing reality and changes. Not only can the reality of implementing a plan highlight deficiencies in the research, it can also reveal errors which perhaps should have been identified earlier. Also, even where the research gives accurate information, circumstances can change.

By using assessment as an ongoing process we were able to develop a more open plan, which allowed not only for doubts during the research phase but also for change as the project developed.

The first doubts were raised during the compilation of the profile of the estate, particularly in respect of the other new initiatives previously mentioned. However, the education centre, though working in the same age range as that identified by the project (0-12), was clearly operating within an educational framework, concentrating on forging links between school and home. Similarly the youth centre did not pose any problems as it would be focusing on the 14+ age group.

The project agreed to try to develop some work with junior youth which could eventually move into the youth centre. Some of the existing resources were struggling: the playgroup had an uncertain future; the playbus was under threat. Information available indicated that there would be no facilities for under 5s in the neighbourhood other than the local authority day nursery which was oversubscribed.

Any doubts soon got submerged in the general enthusiasm of creating something new and in the fact that several decisions had been made: the estate on which we should work, the building in which we would be accommodated and the broad focus of the project's work.

The building was made available in August 1983 and we estimated that it could open as a centre in January 1984. The plan was to use the autumn period to make further contacts with residents and seek ideas from them. Unfortunately, there were several unexpected delays in the development of the building, the recruiting of staff became piecemeal and, once staff were appointed, it was difficult to organise a coherent team development programme.

Within about six months it was becoming apparent that the project was not developing at the pace we had envisaged. The centre had developed activities for under 5s and a junior youth club, both of which had input from the neighbourhood, but in general terms the centre was being used by no more than about a dozen families. This created several pressures. Firstly, concern was being expressed amongst the staff that there was a real danger of a clique forming. Furthermore, there was pressure to spend time attempting to sort out disagreements and petty back biting amongst users. The difficulty in this was that it was hard to separate what stemmed from the centre and what did not. The initial research had taken insufficient account of the potential for this kind of problem. Furthermore, insufficient attention had been given to the increased reluctance of people to commit themselves to communal roles in a social system that provides little by way of rewarding interaction for people with others outside their front doors. "The privatisation of community life has also been accompanied by an increasing disinterest and subsequent ignorance about the lives of those living around one".[2]

The staff appointed to the project had mainly had experience in either youth and community work or teaching experience and consequently did not have the skills to handle these situations. The combination of these two factors was impairing the ability to instigate neighbourhood activities and generally undermining confidence.

Because of the underlying belief that assessment was an ongoing process, the team was able to take stock of the situation. We looked again at the earlier statements of aims, objectives and philosophy. The validity of these statements was re-affirmed but we attempted to make sense of them in the context of what we were experiencing.

Firstly, we sought the help of a consultant to undertake team development. This was a useful exercise. It helped to free staff from inappropriate individual and collective blame for the problems that had been encountered. It also gave us a clearer view of where we could go. We could still hold on to the philosophy and the general aims. What we needed to do was to look again at our objectives.

The process of assessment allowed us to assimilate the realities of working within a neighbourhood, into the overall aims and objectives. Practitioners often have to work within a framework largely defined by others. Few would expect that everything would work out at the first attempt, and projects do require a time to come alongside the neighbourhood.

Assessing the way forward, the team highlighted the need to attempt to have a far wider contact with residents so that the first user groups would be more representative.

We also realised we should have taken more account of the suspicion those already working in the area would feel towards the project. Our approaches to existing groups had been low key in an attempt to allay fears that we would take over small groups. These attempts to reassure did not work and it was a long time before we could have a relationship that was seen as non-threatening to such groups.

An important element in an acceptance of the process of assessment is for the agency to build in the appropriate structures. The use of annual project plans can provide such a structure. It is essential, however, that such plans should involve all staff and also the users.

Our revised strategy built on those aspects of work which were enabling local people to use the resources of the centre effectively. In addition, it enabled the team to look at new areas of interest which warranted investment of time and energy.

We also identified that it was necessary to distinguish the differences between centre-based work and work with the wider neighbourhood. This helped those groups based at the centre to become more independent and led to a debate over what the project should be termed. It had started life being called a family centre, but some users felt that the title carried a stigma, implying you had to have a problem to come to the centre. It was decided that 'neighbourhood project' would be more appropriate.

Slowly, we began to formalise links with other groups, some which were relatively new, which worked with children. Working alongside these groups we were able to form a 'play forum' which would help to represent voluntary work being done on the estate with children. Through this intervention it was hoped that an organisational structure would be developed that would be of benefit to all the groups on the estate.

There are a number of ways in which the work within neighbourhood projects can be subject to continuous assessment. Firstly, the workers themselves can undertake regular assessment. Secondly, it can be encouraged through organisational methods – ie, through line management. Thirdly, projects can use a consultant, outside line management.

In practice the process of assessment should involve all three. The team of workers has to feel that it is part of the process. Management has a responsibility to be aware of the difficulties and to enable workable strategies to be developed as part of the process of assessment. The use of a consultant who is external to the organisation can provide a guided format for reflection and the development of strategies that enable the project process to develop.

An additional advantage of using an external consultant is that he or she can make observations not only on the work of the project but also on the implications of the work and its development for management and for the organisation. In our experience the consultant enabled the team to explore the issues more openly than would have been possible if the whole process of assessment had taken place within the management structure of the agency.

All workers bring their own values, beliefs, aspirations and commitment to a project. It is vital that all these components are taken account of in the development of the project. If the early stages of the project stand the test of practice and experience, the project should develop satisfactorily. It is when gaps are found in these early phases that problems arise.

There is a fine line between a constructive assessment and a destructive one. The reaction for those directly involved in the process is crucial. If assessment is viewed merely as a fact-finding exercise undertaken at a specific time, and if the assessment is seen to carry elements of power and of finality, problems can be seen as failure. On the other hand, if assessment is seen to be a valuable and ongoing process, the team should be less susceptible to negative feelings and should be able to tackle any problems creatively. It should help create a working framework which is flexible without being woolly.

Our experience at Hill Top has been by no means unique. We believe, however, that our view of assessment has provided a positive model and one we would encourage others to adopt.

References

[1]   Phelan J. *Family Centres: a study.* London: The Children's Society, 1983.

[2]   Thomas D N. *The Making of Community Work.* London: George Allen & Unwin, 1983: p95.

Derek Akker has had 20 years' experience of social work and community work, 11 of which were spent working with local authority social service departments, specialising in children and young people. Since joining The Children's Society he has been involved in setting up two neighbourhood projects and is currently running a community advice service. In July 1988 he leaves The Children's Society to become a curate in the Diocese of Manchester.

THE INTER – AGENCY APPROACH

Ruth Hall

This paper aims to discuss inter-agency work, considering why it has been slow to develop in practice in the United Kingdom, and why it could improve the quality and appropriateness of social welfare services for care in the community. The term inter-agency work is used to indicate co-operative and collaborative working in joint initiatives by different agencies, both voluntary and statutory, often with some shared resources, and co-ordinated in a federal structure. The aim of this model of work is to make services more accessible to the communities who use them. This approach has been called community organisation.[1] I will set the development of inter-agency collaboration in the historical context of community work and community social work, and then go on to cite examples of inter-agency work which could provide models for future collaborative work of this type.

In his analysis of the development of community work within the context of social work, Jones suggests there is a continuum, casework, with an emphasis on the individual, being at one end and community work, with an emphasis on collective action in relation to the community, at the other. His definition of community work includes a range of activities such as community organisation, administration and social planning.[2] Conversely, Thomas suggests five approaches (of which community organisation is one) in which community work as an intervention is just one aspect of each approach.

Both the Seebohm (1968) and Barclay (1982) Reports have pointed to the importance of developing inter-agency work within a community framework.[3,4] The Seebohm Report emphasised the importance of integrating services, while the

Barclay Report, in advocating a community social work approach, was in effect repeating many of the Seebohm Report's recommendations. The Barclay Report, by advocating a community approach, acknowledged two important points: firstly, the need for greater involvement in provision of services by the consumers of those services; and, secondly, an awareness of the fact that such an approach could not be fully implemented in social services but would need to include housing, health and education services. The Barclay Report also emphasised the importance of social care planning as a major function of social work, bringing together formal and informal resources to produce social care plans which utilise the services of self-help groups, volunteers, community organisations, and voluntary and statutory agencies. Clearly this type of planning would require inter-agency collaboration.

Despite these recommendations, inter-agency work within a community work setting is not common in the UK, where the emphasis has tended to be on neighbourhood work practised within an agency context. Community social work has also been characterised by the development of 'patch' teams within social services agencies, rather than on an inter-agency basis, and in fact in some instances the 'patch' teams have been restricted in scope to certain groups of workers (usually fieldworkers) within an agency – rather than integrating all groups of the agency's workers.

An early example of inter-agency work in the UK was the Multi-Services Centre, at Vauxhall in Liverpool, which was established in 1972 based on the theory of inter-organisational co-ordination in social welfare as developed by Reid.[5]

The centre's stated objectives were to improve the accessibility and co-ordination of local services and to increase local accountability for and control over those services.[6] It attempted to involve all agencies working in the area and made provision for them to operate from one building. With varying degrees of success the following agencies operated a service from the centre, under the management of a centre or project co-ordinator: social services, probation service, education welfare service, voluntary agencies, health services, careers services, Department of Health and Social Security, the police and environmental health. Thus the centre brought together a wide range of services, which attempted to work co-operatively; furthermore, the workers at the centre began to see themselves as a group working to help the area, rather than as individual employees of an agency.

Another, rather different, example of inter-agency collaboration has been established for the local community at the Dukeries Complex in Nottinghamshire. A comprehensive school found that its numbers were falling and that some of its resources were therefore being underused. A group which involved the local community as well as the professionals concerned undertook a study to identify how these resources should be used. The resulting complex is a community resource, which is a federation of separate units comprising: the original comprehensive school (now a community college); a recreation centre; an under 5s centre with a social services drop-in centre; a community library; a youth centre; an information centre and mini town hall; a day centre for the elderly; a residential centre for courses; and a social education centre for the mentally handicapped. All units share a belief in co-operation for mutual benefit and in participative, responsive and holistic management; all have common aims to promote the quality of life and to promote access, confidence, and interaction. Thus the complex is an example of inter-agency co-operation which has benefited all members of the local community.

A closer examination of Reid's theoretical approach[5] indicates that there are distinct advantages to be gained from developing inter-agency work. His theory is based on the notion that agencies collaborate on the basis of an exchange of resources to achieve their goals. These resources may be tangible – such as funds and personnel – or intangible – such as prestige. Further, his basic premise is that collaboration is a function of whether agencies are independent, interdependent, or in a state of conflict with one another, and that it is most likely to occur where they are interdependent. Interdependent agencies need to exchange resources in order to better achieve their goals, and their interdependence is likely to be greater the more similar are their goals. Other factors identified as facilitating agency collaboration are: crises, which may increase interdependence, as in some of the current work being undertaken with AIDS; the existing level of communication between agencies, as with the examples of inter-agency work in Kirklees discussed below; and where collaboration increases the ability to achieve goals and at the same time is cost effective. The historical changes which have led The Children's Society to develop its work in neighbour-hoods in a community social work context are documented by the Editor in his introduction. He also poses the question of whether this interest is being led to some extent by the availability of resources. The same question can be raised about the examples of inter-agency collaboration, largely initiated by the voluntary sector, which I shall give. Has the motivation for this collaborative work been resources – particularly financial – expediency, expertise, or a combination of all three? Whatever the reason, I would like to demonstrate by these examples of inter-agency work that the achievements of their collaborative work are potentially greater than those of the individual agencies.

The Children's Society has begun to be involved in inter-agency work; two examples of this work have been in Kirklees. The first was a project for adolescent girls in care known as the Kirklees Project for Girls, developed jointly by Kirklees Social Services Department, Barnardo's and The Children's Society. The social services department had identified that the needs of this particular group were not being met by existing resources, thus supporting Reid's theory that agencies collaborate on the basis of an exchange of resources. The project's aim was to prepare the adolescent girls for independent living when they left care. Each of the three agencies were able to provide resources: social services provided a residential unit; The Children's Society provided independent living units; Barnardo's provided specialist foster parents. Barnardo's also provided a project leader to co-ordinate and manage these resources. In some respects this project provides another example of a federal structure. Although this collaboration was not precipitated by a crisis situation as described by Reid the project clearly filled a gap in existing resources and its development was facilitated by the existing communication between the two voluntary child care agencies. The initial funding for this inter-agency project came from the DHSS – for three years subsequently extended to four – on the condition that the project was managed by a voluntary agency. This raises the issue concerning the motivation for inter-agency collaboration discussed earlier. However, this project has now been absorbed into local authority mainstream funding, and remains as an integrated unit managed by one worker. This is some indication of its success as an innovative inter-agency initiative to resource unmet needs. Reid's theory about the advantages of the exchange of tangible and intangible resources in inter-agency projects is borne out by an evaluation of the Kirklees project. The combined experience, expertise and training resources of the three agencies extended their ability to develop creative ways of working in an innovative project; and the development of trust and open communication between the three agencies increased their interdependence.

The second example of inter-agency work in Kirklees was to some extent facilitated by the experience of the Kirklees Project for Girls. The basis of interdependence and increased levels of communication had already been established by the agencies involved in the project (with one exception). The project, known as the Kirklees Enterprise for Youth (KEY), was established to provide a community-based alternative to custody and care for juveniles in Kirklees. The agencies involved were The Children's Society, Barnardo's, the National Children's Centre and Kirklees Social Services Department, who employed the worker responsible for the management and co-ordination of the project. Again the funding came from central government under the DHSS LAC(83)3 initiative, through the voluntary sector, but the local authority contributed funding to this project from the outset, and absorbed it into mainstream local authority funding when the initial central government funding expired.

KEY was a complex example of inter-agency collaboration. Each of the three voluntary agencies had a separate project, which together provided a range of flexible alternatives to custody and care. Each project had a distinct target group but their resources were used flexibly between agencies from the outset. Ultimately it aimed to establish itself as an integral part of provision for these juveniles throughout Kirklees and to encourage an inter-agency and multi-disciplinary approach to work with them.

The exchange of resources was a significant feature in the development of the KEY project. At the planning stage the representation of all interested agencies (extending beyond those directly involved in KEY) helped to ensure that KEY was a collaborative venture involving interested parties throughout Kirklees.

The role of the project manager and three project leaders in co-ordinating and allocating work between the projects underlined the importance of inter-agency agreement and co-operation. Resources and personnel were always used flexibly between the agencies involved in KEY – for example, group workers moved between the separate projects as demand required and joint training was provided, drawing on the wider resources of the four agencies involved. The shared experience undoubtedly led to greater inter-agency co-operation within KEY; and this extended beyond the scheme, underlining the importance of collaboration in work with juveniles in their own community after they had left KEY. Examples of this have been increased co-operation with the education department and schools, and with workers in statutory agencies responsible for supervision orders in respect of these juveniles.

Reid discusses the role of the co-ordinating agency in facilitating interdependence in inter-agency work. In both the Kirklees examples the role of the project co-ordinator – employed by Barnardo's in Kirklees Project for Girls and by social services in KEY – was instrumental in ensuring co-operation and collaboration between the agencies involved.

In this way Reid underlines the importance of the co-ordinator's leadership and communication skills in achieving clarity of goals and efficient use of resources. Where the co-ordinator is unable to facilitate interdependence Reid goes on to discuss 'inducing' that interdependence on the basis of control over resources and power. Where the co-ordinator has access to resources which other agencies need, he/she may use these to create interdependence between the agencies. For example, the co-ordinating agency may have funds which can be allocated on the basis of exchange with other agencies provided that the funding is used in specific ways. This in turn will facilitate interdependence between agencies on the basis of shared goals in the use of these funds. Alternatively, the co-ordinator may induce interdependence through the use of power or influence. This is usually achieved through the co-ordinating agency's relationships with those individuals or organisations which have formal authority over the agencies being co-ordinated. This use of resources and power by the co-ordinator was not something that occurred in either the Kirklees Project for Girls or KEY example discussed above.

The Children's Society has been instrumental in developing inter-agency collaboration in a rather different role in the borough of St Helens. In this case, the focus has been more on involving the local community in the development of a relevant service for children's play. This development has arisen out of The Children's Society's work with two family and community centres in St Helens, and a recognition by the borough's Community Leisure Department of the positive role played by The Children's Society in the development of community associations and of the partnership relationship between the local authority, voluntary projects, and local communities.

This concurs with Reid's notion of the exchange of intangible resources – in this instance the prestige and reputation of The Children's Society in this area of work in St Helens. The result has been the establishment of a project which will promote the concept of partnership between voluntary agencies, statutory agencies and community groups throughout St Helens to facilitate the development of co-ordinated and comprehensive services for children's play. The project will use its existing contacts and reputation in St Helens to fulfil a co-ordinating role in new developments in relation to children and their welfare.

I have attempted to demonstrate that there are clear advantages to be gained from inter-agency collaboration – both for the agencies concerned and for the consumers of their services. In summary these are as follows:

– The complementary nature of the work, particularly in the case of voluntary agencies, allows for a range of skills and resources to be pooled between agencies with the potential of increasing both the effectiveness of the service and the learning for all involved.

– Collaborative models of working, again particularly where voluntary agencies are involved, have the potential to develop a different relationship with the users of the services provided. The boundaries between the helped and the helper become more blurred and there is a greater potential for sharing power with the users of services.

- The range of influence of inter-agency projects – in terms of raising consciousness and increasing public awareness – is potentially greater than that of a single agency. This influence can operate both locally and nationally, as in the case of the KEY project in Kirklees. At a local level juvenile justice practice and policies on the use of custody and care for juveniles have been influenced in all the agencies involved. At a national level the experiences of the KEY scheme have contributed to the debate concerning the abolition of custody for juveniles.

- The nature of the funding of both Kirklees Project for Girls and KEY enabled the individual voluntary agencies involved to engage in innovatory work that may not have been possible for them individually. In addition, it can be an advantage for small voluntary agencies to spread the risks associated with securing funds by engaging in collaborative work.

There can also be disadvantages to inter-agency work. This is particularly true if the co-ordinating role is not managed effectively, when the individual agencies may compete against each other for funding or resources, and the loyalty of the workers may be to their own agency rather than to the collaborative venture. Again Reid's theory about communication and shared goals is relevant here. The different agencies involved in collaborative work may each have different policies and procedures, particularly in relation to their staff, which can create problems if co-ordination is not managed sensitively. This was a potential source of conflict in the KEY project which was managed successfully by the overall project manager and co-ordinator. A further disadvantage for local community groups may be that if they are not involved in the collaborative work they may find themselves facing a quasi-monopoly and be excluded from influencing the development of local community resources.

I would suggest that these disadvantages are in the main avoidable, but the role of the co-ordinator in facilitating interdependence between the agencies involved in collaborative work is crucial. If this role is undertaken successfully, the potential advantages of inter-agency collaboration are considerable and can outweigh the possible disadvantages.

The examples given of The Children's Society's involvement in inter-agency work all differ in degree and in the extent to which they engage in partnership with the local community. The projects in Kirklees are concerned mainly with the delivery of statutory services, and the focus of the collaborative work is between large voluntary agencies and the relevant statutory agencies. In St Helens the Society's role is concerned more with the co-ordination of small voluntary organisations and community groups, with partnership with local communities, and with the relationship between all of these and the statutory agencies in St Helens. None of these examples have achieved the degree of collaboration shown at the Multi-Services Centre in Vauxhall. However, their success as innovative projects form a basis of knowledge and experience from which future collaborative work could be developed.

This leaves The Children's Society with the opportunity to develop this potential and to build on its experience of collaborative work. It can then develop further the community approach to work, which will provide the basis for a practice theory built on the experience of both workers and users. One way forward may be to link the experience of both inter-agency work and the development of local control. Two of the three examples of inter-agency work in this chapter have involved collaboration between professional agencies and their workers. In the case of The Children's Society, however, this work has embodied the philosophy of empowerment, although users were not directly involved in project management.

Where The Children's Society has been involved in the development of local control, referred to by the Editor and others here, there has been more active participation by users in the management of projects.

In future The Children's Society may combine these two models of practice to influence the development of inter-agency collaborative work. For example, the Society may undertake the co-ordinating role to obtain the secondment of workers from a number of agencies to work to a local management committee. This could lead to the establishment of a range of locally based services, provided collaboratively, at the same time as increasing consumer choice and the power of local communities to determine both the type and means of provision of services. This model would harness the advantages of inter-agency work as discussed above. However, it is equally important to maintain a balance, to avoid a quasi-monopoly in which sections of the community would be excluded from representation in the local management of resources and services thereby actually reducing choice for some individuals. Equally, if the local management group controls the provision of all local services, this may reduce choice by offering no alternatives where these local services do not meet needs. Clearly the future development of inter-agency work will take various forms, but The Children's Society is well placed to develop models of the type discussed above on the basis of its existing experience.

References

1   Thomas D N. *The Making of Community Work.* London: Allen and Unwin, 1983: Ch 3.

2   Jones D. Community work in the United Kingdom. In: Specht H and Vickery A. *Integrating Social Work Methods.* London: Allen and Unwin, 1977.

3   *Report of the Committee on Local Authority and Allied Personal Social Services* (Chairman: Lord Seebohm). London: HMSO, 1968.

4   Working Party of National Institute for Social Work (Chairman: P Barclay). *Social Workers: Their Roles and Tasks.* London: Bedford Square Press, 1982.

5   Reid W J. Inter-organisational co-ordination in social welfare: a theoretical approach to analysis and intervention. In: Kramer and Specht (eds). *Readings in Community Organisations' Practice.* New York: Prentice Hall, 1969

6   Topping P and Smith G. *Government Against Poverty.*
     Final Report of Liverpool Community Development
     Programme. Liverpool: CDP, 1977 (see also Open
     University Course DE 206. *Community Work in Practice
     2,* units 17-19 part 1).

*Ruth Hall has worked as a social worker, as a senior lecturer,
and in staff development and training. She currently works as
a consultant for The Children's Society and as a freelance
consultant and researcher.*

STARTING A PROJECT WITH EVALUATION IN MIND

Neil Proctor and Jenny Sayer

The period between the appointment of a worker in a community project and the completion of the first major report (the entry phase) is crucial. It is during this period that decisions are made about the work to be undertaken, and the intentions of the project are demonstrated by the methods used to make contact with people and to develop understanding of the area. Case studies of community projects often identify the entry phase as a time of confusion and uncertainty for the worker who may be expected to make sense of someone else's vision rather than to work to a clear job description.[1,2] In this paper we attempt to show how beginning a project with evaluation in mind provides a clear basis for decision making, makes the work of the entry phase much more systematic and has direct practical outcomes.

In the project about which this article is written, the South Bank Project, several factors facilitated the reflection on practice that is a necessary part of the process of evaluation. Firstly, before The Children's Society had decided to develop work in the area they had gathered relevant information about the area and had negotiated at length with other agencies and organisations (as outlined by Peter Wiggin, pp 56-70). Secondly, the original project proposal contained a clearly identified community development approach: 'working alongside and with families and groups in the community, rather than with families on a treatment basis.' It included a commitment to the principles of participation, prevention and shared responsibility. Thirdly, the Society's management recognised the need not only to appoint an experienced community development worker but also to provide structured support for that worker. This included the involvement of a community work consultant, who took part in the initial interviews of candidates and thereafter met with the worker monthly. Fourthly, the agency recognised that reflection and analysis were a vital part of the development of the project. This recognition validated thinking and analysis as a necessary part of the job, thus considerably reducing the pressure on the worker to take action at the expense of reflection – a pressure commonly felt by community workers.

Following the appointment of the project leader, he and the consultant began to gather and analyse information on the area, as is customary at the beginning of most community projects.[3] The integration of evaluation at this stage, however, had specific implications. Firstly, it forced us to define what we meant by 'community project'. Secondly, the nature of the questions asked during the research phase had to be developed beyond the relatively simple framework of identifying needs and resources.[4] Thirdly, we had to develop methods of collating the information gained which not only facilitated immediate analysis but would also lay the foundation (the baseline) for later evaluation.

Defining the project

Before we could begin to establish criteria to assess effectiveness, it was necessary to define what we meant by a community project. This may sound obvious, but those familiar with current debates about family centres will know that this is a difficult issue;[5] 'family' is often defined as 'mothers with small children' while 'centre' is seen as synonymous with 'a building'. Many projects take their identity from a target group (under 5s, for example) or from specific activities (such as welfare rights). Although the activities are obviously necessary, they need to be framed within a wider concept of what they are attempting to achieve.

A further clarification is necessary where a community development approach is adopted. The term 'community' is currently used in social welfare in two ways: the Association of Community Workers, for example, uses it to define a way of working which promotes equality, participation and empowerment. Alternatively, for example in the 'patch' system of social work, it is used to define a geographical boundary. It can also be used functionally – for example, in the expression 'the residential community'. The variations in the use of the terms often create confused expectations – particularly in joint-funded projects – and can lead to the selection of vague, inconsistent or irrelevant criteria for evaluation.

If these problems are to be avoided, the worker has to develop a framework for action which specifies the way the term 'community' is being used. In the case of South Bank several factors influenced the development of this framework. Firstly, the original geographical focus was town-wide (based on ward and parish boundaries). Secondly, the sponsoring agency was The Children's Society, so we clearly could not focus on the elderly. Thirdly, there was a commitment to participation and local control, so a service delivery model was not acceptable. Fourthly, the consultant had developed the concept of 'field of practice' to represent not only the activities and events in a community project but also the ways in which a project influences and recreates the concepts and practice of social life.[6] A project working with unemployed people, for example, would not see its work only in terms of activities to help them to occupy their unused time; it would also aim to change ideas and practices about work within the wider society, including those adopted by people who are employed and by those responsible for policy-making affecting unemployment – that is, the field of practice related to unemployment. Using the concept of 'field of practice' to define a project means that, during the entry phase of a project, a worker has to examine not only the activities, resources and needs in the area but also the attitudes, behaviour and understanding which have created them.

The South Bank project eventually began with a definition of community as 'a functional and social system related to the care and development of children'. 'System' here refers to the combination of beliefs, attitudes and practices which together make up the context in which children develop. For example, ideas about parenting as held by formal structures such as schools and health services may define how teachers behave towards parents, whether a child is taken into care, and levels of welfare benefits advocated. The ideas of good parenting held by local people may reinforce and/or be reinforced by those of the formal system or may differ considerably. The interaction of ideas and practices, of informal and formal parts of the system, will influence the lives of children in an area and will have an impact on perceptions of parenting held by the wider community.[7] The project was then defined from this concept of community as 'a set of resources and interventions which aim to create specific changes in attitudes and related practices within the specific field of the child development system' (see figure 1).

The work of the entry phase was to explore and understand this system of practice with a view to developing specific and relevant targets for change, with their corresponding criteria for evaluation.

Investigating the field of practice

When community development has evolved in the context of social work it has traditionally been based on a response-to-needs model[8] and has focused on a geographical area.[9] Questions are asked about existing needs and the project will set out to meet those needs. This approach often results in projects being established in areas of great stress, with little realistic analysis of how a comparatively small input of resources might alleviate those needs. It can also lead to a 'patching up' of an existing bad situation or to the neglect of external factors which influence and create internal problems.[10] The South Bank project modified this concept of community development. The modification had direct implications for the way in which we investigated the field of practice.

Figure 1 - A model for action

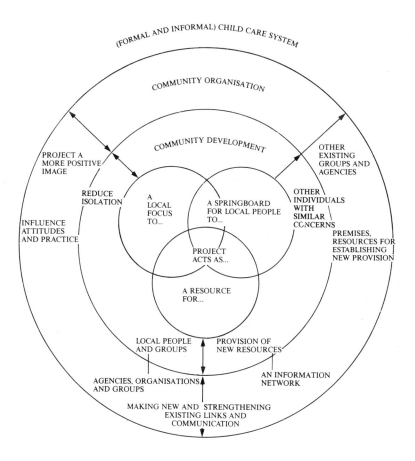

In the first place (and in common with a response-to-needs model) we had to gather information about the area. We did this by collating statistics, mapping the environment and its resources, and identifying existing organisations and activities. The bibliography shows the books and papers which we found most useful at this stage.

Because of our definition of community, however, we also had to develop ways of analysing attitudes and practices relating to the development of children. For example, we took account of the fact that the way in which organisations and groups define the people with whom they work – 'clients', 'mums', 'my babies' – affects the way in which workers behave towards those people . It also affects people's responses to the agencies and how they see themselves ('we're all dead-legs here'). Figure 2 shows the major categories used in this part of the investigation.

It is important at this stage to recognise three things about what we were trying to do. Firstly, the information we wanted to collect was the sort of information normally gathered informally and was not easily turned into data. Secondly, another project with another field of practice would need to develop its own relevant methods of collating information. The principle is one of collecting relevant information and turning it into data.[11] Thirdly, the collection of information was an ongoing process rather than a series of discrete, specific acts. As such, we had to accept that it was a live process, one which could instigate change in its own right – for example, exchanging information about existing resources can itself change their use. We had to record the impact of our research as well as information obtained through it.

Developing methods of recording and analysis

As we collected the information, we began to understand the interrelationship between various components of the field of practice. Each set of information had to be compared and contrasted in order to identify patterns and to confirm or refute hypotheses based on the original social profile.

Figure 2 – Component parts of field of practice

Local agencies, organisations and groups
Whom they serve (catchment area/interest group)
How they are organised
Attitudes to other organisations, agencies, groups
Attitudes to local people and children
How they view South Bank (strengths and weaknesses)
Their style of interaction with other organisations/agencies
Their style of interaction with local people

Local people
Boundaries of South Bank
Internal division in township
Attitudes to organisations, agencies and groups (general and specific)
Attitudes to other local people/children
Resources required – where, what and for whom
Strengths and weaknesses of community

Local children
Boundaries of South Bank
More localised neighbourhoods/areas
How they view organisations and groups – which they know of/ use/
don't use
How they view peers, parents, etc
Alternative resources
What they view as positive/negative about South Bank
Resources they feel the area requires

Resources
Where sited
Level of use
Availability
Gaps identified
Cost
Who uses them (catchment area/interest group)

Image
How local people, groups, agencies, children view South Bank
How outsiders view South Bank
How South Bank is portrayed in the media
Images of selves and others

For example, we plotted existing resources in South Bank on an acetate sheet and then plotted local area statistics relating to social indicators such as car ownership and population structure, on a separate sheet. When one sheet was overlaid on the other it was evident that one specific geographical area was very isolated from existing resources and facilities and also had the lowest car ownership. This information affected our decision about the location of a building for the project and thus made the geographical focus of the area more specific.

Identification of patterns was only one aim of the analysis. We were also concerned to lay the foundation for later evaluation. This concern led us to gather our findings under specific headings which could be used, in conjunction with listed targets for change and their related indicators, for future evaluation (for examples see figure 3).

A major report based on this information was produced and circulated to sponsoring agencies and other interested parties, particularly those involved in the research. The report analysed and evaluated the entry phase and outlined targets for the next phase of the project, moving towards direct engagement with local people. It identified two major focuses for the work: development of resources in a specific neighbourhood; and town-wide co-ordination and exchange of information within the child development system.

At the end of the entry phase we had identified clear benefits to using this approach. Firstly, we had devised an ongoing file of information on the area, available to all interested parties (having due regard to confidentiality of some information). More particularly, there was information on the organisations involved with children, and their resources, which should help the co-ordination of activities and future developments. Analysis of the available resources enabled the project to decide that the purchase of a minibus would be useful and would demonstrate a commitment to the co-ordinating role.

Figure 3 – Targets for change with related indicators (examples)

Target	*Indicator*
The development of greater communication and co-ordination between groups, organisations and agencies and local people in South Bank.	Improved communication through newsletters, information sheets advertising, reaching more people. An increase in the use of organisations by individuals in the area would be an indicator. The outcome of providing information to either local people or organisations would be recorded. Recording initiatives made by the project (eg, directory/newsletters) to facilitate this development.
An improvement in resources available to babies and children under 16, including an improvement in the play facilities and provision in South Bank.	Recording and monitoring project involvement or initiation in developments. This could include existence of more youth groups, provision of new resources (eg, toy library, minibus), development of umbrella organisations such as under 5s, or play forum, and provision of creative play opportunities.
Create a more positive image of South Bank to those outside the township.	A project as small as this one can only hope to influence this marginally. However, by promoting the positive work being done in and by the community with 'outsiders' and providing positive copy for the local media some impact could be made. The evidence for a shift to be monitored through newspaper cuttings, recording impressions of the township and recording local groups, attitude to positive selling.

The development of stronger links, communication and involvement between the Redcar Road East Estate and the rest of South Bank.	This would be indicated by the increased involvement of adults and children from the estate in activities and resources elsewhere in South Bank, and by people from elsewhere in South Bank in activities on the estate; this would be systematically recorded.
The recognition of the skills and potential of residents of Redcar Road East Estate by individuals, agencies, groups and organisations from other parts of South Bank.	The project's involvement with local people in achieving goals and ensuring these are known widely. Monitoring and recording interaction resulting from achievements that demonstrate recognition.

The need to set specific targets, with related criteria for evaluation, led to a disciplined approach to decision making about work to be undertaken. It had to be related to a clear time framework[12] which took account of new people and systems which would become involved as the project grew. The worker developed a clear understanding of the function and focus of the project and as a result felt more confident in negotiations with other agencies.

The specific definition of the field of practice meant the recognition of the importance of the children's experience of South Bank. Thus we made an effort to ascertain and analyse children's opinions and ideas. This process radically altered some identified targets for change and reinforced others – it confirmed the isolation of the estate, for example, but made play resources a much higher priority.

Some aspects of the methodology raised rather more controversial issues. Much of the initial work was carried out with agencies and organisations (within the formal parts of the systems) which is contrary to much community development practice. Our particular definition of community, however, required the development of an understanding of existing attitudes and practices (as well as activities and resources) which influenced children's lives and opportunities in order to be able to identify a realistic and relevant role for the project and to avoid duplication of effort. The second phase of the project, involving a second worker, will concentrate on the informal system and eventually will modify the initial analysis. Another project, perhaps more locally based, might adopt a different sequence of investigation and methodology while eventually ending up with similar categories of information.

As we distinguished between formal and informal systems, however, we became less sure about the traditional division between local people and organisations in community work. The more significant division in South Bank was between those involved in and/or using resources and those cut off from them geographically or socially. For example, are professionals necessarily outsiders? Is someone who used to live in the area but now commutes a local person? Is the most relevant criterion one of feeling you belong to and have an investment in the area?

We have already referred to two other specific changes in thinking as a result of starting with evaluation in mind. Firstly, we changed from structuring the analysis on the basis of need, to structuring it on the basis of potential for change. This led us to focus on areas with potential strengths rather than those with the most need. Secondly, our definition of 'community' moved from being exclusively geographical and social to include function and interest, and this tried to recognise the actual and potential conflicts of interest.

A third change, not previously mentioned, should also be noted. We moved from a concept of work as task orientated and the workers as action centred to a concept of work as process orientated and the worker as facilitator/enabler. Because community projects are often located in areas of highest devastation and depression community work is often seen as short-term relief of immediate circumstances. There is immense pressure on projects to respond to every crisis. By developing a high profile for evaluation from the beginning, we found we had to recognise the importance and relevance of setting boundaries for action and establishing criteria for making constructive choices. We learnt to value thinking and analysis as much as direct action. We had to develop criteria for evaluation of the process of the work (changes in personal and social interaction) as well as for the activities. For example, we needed to be able to assess changes in relationships between parents and professionals as well as to identify the number of parents attending specific groups. We had also to develop long-term analysis into which short-term action could be built (to answer questions such as 'what, why, is it possible?').

The impact of evaluation on the development of the project has – we hope – been shown clearly. Having established a baseline we should find that when evaluation is required for funding or planning this can be undertaken quickly and incisively.

The clear sense of direction has certainly given the workers greater confidence and should result in a steady development without the problems created by attempts to meet unrealistic expectations. It has provided support during one of the most uncertain and challenging stages of any project. However, we still need to ask 'Is this the right approach?'

The answer will depend on the concept of community work being used. If community work is seen as a short-term strategy for alleviating the worst of society's ills, or as a method of control through informal education, or as compensation for lack of resources, then the slow entry phase could be seen as a waste of time. The theory on which we based our work was that a slow systematic entry phase would enable a more rapid and effective take-off, avoid duplication of activity and facilitate a contribution to real change. There is some evidence that this has been happening in South Bank.

Many of the benefits, however, will not be evident until later in the project's development. All we can say at the moment is that integrating evaluation into the work of the project from the start has been a constructive experience for those involved and has contributed to the effectiveness of the project's work in its early stages.

References

1 Williamson H. *Dilemmas of a Project Worker.* Unpublished paper. The Children's Society (Banbury Project) 1986.

2 Harlesden Community Project. *Community Work and Caring for Children: a community project in an inner city local authority.* Ilkley: Owen Wells, 1979: pp 3-7.

3 Stone W. *Identifying Social Need.* London: The Children's Society, 1981.

4 Hedley R. *Measuring Success: a Guide to Evaluation for Voluntary & Community Groups.* London: Advance, 1985.

5 De'Ath E. *Self-help and Family Centres; a current initiative in helping the community.* London: National Children's Bureau, 1985.

6 Sayer J. *How Does the Ideology of the Community Worker Affect Community Practice?* Unpublished M. Phil Thesis, Lancaster University 1985: pp 143-155.

7 Hasler J. *Family Centres – Different Expressions, same principles.* London: The Children's Society, 1983.

8 Sayer J. Ideology: the bridge between theory and practice. *Community Development Journal* 1986: Vol 21 No 4: pp 294-303.

9 Henderson P and Thomas D N. *Skills in Neighbourhood Work.* London: Allen & Unwin, 1983.

10 Alinsky S D. *Rules for Radicals: a practical primer for realistic radicals.* New York: Random House, 1971.

11 Cain M. and Finch J. Towards a rehabilitation of data. In: Abrams P D, et al. *Practice and Progress: British Sociology, 1950-1980.* London: Allen and Unwin, 1981: pp 105-119.

12 Association of Community Workers. *The Community Workers' Manual.* London: ACW, 1979: section 8.5.

Bibliography

Glampson A, Stott T, Thomas D N. *A Guide to the Assessment of Community Needs and Resources.* London: National Institute for Social Work, 1975.

Moser C A. and Kalton G. *Survey Methods in Social Investigation.* 2nd ed. London: Heinemann Educational, 1971: pp 40; 238; 302.

Parlett M. Illuminative evaluation. In: Rowan J and Reason P (ed). *Human Inquiry: A Sourcebook of New Paradigm Research.* Chichester: John Wiley and Sons, 1981.

Phillips D. *Do it yourself surveys: A hand book for beginners.* London: Polytechnic of North London, Survey Research Clinic, 1981.

Patton M Q. *Qualitative Evaluation Methods.* Beverly Hills, California: Sage, 1980.

Bell C and Newby H. *Community Studies.* London: Allen and Unwin, 1971.

Liffman M. *Power for the Poor: the family centre experiment – an experiment in self help.* London: Allen and Unwin, 1978.

Neil Proctor has worked for three years in The Children's Society South Bank Community Project and previously spent 10 years in various forms of youth and community work in the Cleveland area.

Jenny Sayer is Senior Lecturer in Applied Social Studies at Lancashire Polytechnic, and for the past three years has been working half-time for The Children's Society as a consultant to some of their community projects.

COMMUNITY DEVELOPMENT AND THE ORGANISATION

Ian Sparks

One of my favourite images in describing the way in which the Society's work has developed in the past ten years is that of the Victorian explorer. Livingstone, Stanley and others set out to explore Africa with maps which had full details of the main ports and the rivers which had already been explored, but left blank space for vast tracts of land which were literally off the map.

In the same way the Society's development in the past ten years has taken us off the map in terms of what we knew about how a voluntary organisation should operate. Initially it seemed that these explorations were only about *practice* as we moved from baby adoption and day care to explore family centres and neighbourhood work. However, as the new practice developed, we realised that it was beginning to establish *principles* which affected the way in which the Society was organised and managed.

For example, a community development approach requires you to work in ways which:

- value people rather than devaluing them by focusing on their vulnerability. This has implications for the message conveyed in advertising and publicity material.

- give people access to decision-making processes rather than keeping these processes inside the organisation. This clearly raises questions about how decisions are made.

– focus on responding to the concerns of local people rather than providing a standard package of services agreed with the local authority. This affects the planning process.

These principles raised a number of questions about the management and organisation of the Society and the rest of this paper focuses on these questions.

What sort of organisation are we?

Many charities which have been set up in the last thirty years find that even in this short time their founding statement and public image have ceased to represent what is really happening in the organisation today. Certainly this is true for The Children's Society which was founded in 1881 with the title 'Church of England Incorporated Society for Providing Homes for Waifs and Strays'.

The statement as to what sort of organisation we are is important both for the people who work for the Society and for those who support it. In trying to make our current purpose clear we have to look at two areas:

1) Our Victorian forbears had a certainty about who they were helping (Waifs and Strays) and how (providing homes). This certainty guaranteed their public appeal and developed the sort of image which is still strong with supporters of children's charities. If we are to achieve equal support for, and an equal understanding of, our current vision we have to find a way to explain that building communities, helping people to become mature and responsible, and working in partnership are aims as important as those of rescuing waifs and strays.

2) As we become aware of the need to see children in the context of their families, and families in the context of their communities, there is a natural reaction against an agency remit which limits our work to children and young people up to the age of 25. For some staff it is a natural move to become a family or community organisation on the basis that secure

families or strong communities will ultimately benefit children. My own view is that being The *Children's* Society offers a focus for working in families and communities which would be lost if we became a more general organisation.

Ordinary people are becoming increasingly aware of and concerned about the needs of children. Often these needs are defined in problem terms – sexual abuse, delinquency, divorce – and the layperson's response is equally specific and problem-focused. If we do not make it clear that our community-based work is directly concerned with these issues there is a danger that our work will be discarded as irrelevant.

Why are people giving us their money?

People give money to a charity for a whole variety of reasons – it's well known; a friend asks and you owe them a favour; there's a social expectation; it's part of your lifestyle. Underlying most of these reasons is the expectation that the charity will achieve something; people like to support a cause that works. This is reflected in the fact that the list of top fundraising charities is dominated by famine relief, medical and wildlife charities all of which can offer clear, specific statements about value for money.

However, I believe that people will support the type of work described in this book if we can interpret our work in terms of their concerns. This involves the following points:

1) Language
Supporters are rightly suspicious of jargon – computer salesmen use it to sell you the wrong equipment so might not community workers use it to sell you a useless project? I have had to learn that although the idea of people being oppressed and devalued is a powerful concept, in both community work and Christian terms, the average supporter finds it neither attractive nor compelling. The problem is not their lack of concern for fellow human beings, but their mistrust of what they see as sociological jargon.

In 1986 we launched our first video for supporters about one of our alternatives to custody programmes. This is an area of work which traditional supporters often find difficult to understand and so we worked extra hard at making the message clear without compromising our commitment to stating that locking up young people was wrong and a waste of time. The video has had an enthusiastic response from all audiences including those who previously believed that the 'short, sharp shock' was the only way to combat delinquency.

2) Common experience
Most people know from their own experience that growth and development (whether of a child or of a relationship) is a slow process with many setbacks along the way. The same is true of our community development work. This shared understanding of what life is really like can be the basis for a growing understanding of community-based work.

3) Images
Emotive words like need, weakness and helplessness, which are commonplace in charity advertising, have to be replaced by ideas concerned with building up, growth and ability. From discussions with our advertising agency I know how difficult it is to portray these new ideas in one line on a poster or 100 words in a press advert while still holding on to simple language and a common experience. Any survey of the public image of children's charities shows that they are still associated with adoption and orphanages, mainly, I believe, because the visual and emotional images of those two services are so powerful. So far no-one has found an equally powerful image for community development.

What part do we play in the social services scene?

Voluntary organisations are reaching the point where their part in the total picture of personal social services is beginning to be taken seriously by central and local government. This has been the result of many years' work and is already showing benefits in joint planning and the elimination of duplication. But this co-operation also has disadvantages.

The statutory bodies come to this joint approach with their own agenda about the role which voluntary organisations will play. As they also have access to considerable funds they

naturally feel that this gives them power in defining
nature of the joint work. Those organisations which
dependent on successful negotiations with central or local
government for the majority of their funding have to
compromise and get the best solution possible. The Children's
Society is in the fortunate position that over half of its
income comes from donations (more than £10 million in
1986) and so is unconstrained.

There are obvious advantages in this. Some of the projects
described in this book only started because the Society was
able to use its own money. In other projects the fact that the
Society was contributing to the costs provided a useful lever
in discussions with local authorities – for example, as to why
a neighbourhood centre with open access would be a better
option than a day care centre which only accepted referrals.

What is the appropriate support system?

The process of development which is described in this book
clearly changes the planning focus of the organisation and in
turn changes the focus of the management and support
systems. If projects are planned at local level and developed
as part of a true local partnership, then the local managers
become the lens which focuses the Society's energy on one
spot rather than operatives carrying out a pre-determined
plan.

In this system regionalisation ceases to be a management
structure – fashionable at the moment but liable to be
replaced by a newer fashion – and becomes the necessary
context for community-based planning and management to
take place.

Once this begins to happen there is a natural tendency to
wonder whether the national agency has any role to play or
whether the organisation should not become a loose coalition
of local projects. There are reasons (apart from self-interest)
for maintaining the national context but these are only valid
if they are held in balance with the local context.

As a national body the Society is able to offer:

–   a focus and national identity for donors. While some
     companies and individuals want to give to locally

identifiable work there are many people who identify with and trust national and well-known charities more than local groups.

- a context for the organisation's local work. Many small community projects have uncertain funding which depends on local political conditions. Some inner-city areas have experienced a stream of community projects which have only lasted a short time because either the money ran out or they were under-resourced and the staff burnt out. A national organisation can offer stability and security as well as the feeling that the project is part of a developing pattern of work, not merely the vision of a few enthusiasts.
- a structure for analysis. Community-based work is an unending activity which can take over people's lives. There is so much to do in so little time that standing back to analyse the work can seem a waste of time. The result of this is unfocused work and exhaustion. The Society tries to offer a number of opportunities for analysis. The simplest is the regular staff meeting with a real agenda (not just administration); others include local and regional discussion forums, annual planning statements and three-yearly evaluations including local input. There is a variety of systems for dealing with these; the important thing is to ensure that analysis is planned and sanctioned and does take place.

These national systems only have a value if they are balanced with strong regional activity and the middle manager (assistant regional directors in our terms) plays a strong role in project development. Traditionally middle managers have played a relatively weak role in social service organisations with their main task being one of monitoring and controlling activities which are in the day-to-day control of a more junior manager (the officer-in-charge). In fact the middle manager has a crucial role once the focus changes from the passive role of monitoring to the positive one of applying skills in analysing development issues to both the individual project and the organisation.

If the project is truly committed to responsiveness and development it needs someone to help it analyse its progress in these areas. While an external consultant is an attractive (but expensive) option, the skilled middle manager can offer this analysis with the bonus of a greater understanding of the project and agency ethos, and access to thinking in other parts of the organisation. At the same time the middle manager is able to integrate this work with interventions to outside agencies and to more senior managers.

Externally their focus is on developing understanding about the project's work and re-negotiating agreements so that growth is not hampered. Internally the understanding that comes from working in this way with a number of community projects provides a basis for developing agency policies and identifying ways ahead for practice and management.

Conclusion

To return to my original illustration, one response to this might be to say "I'm quite content with the maps I have. I'll limit myself to the world I understand." This is understandable because exploring new territory is demanding and sometimes only reveals cul-de-sacs. I continue to believe that the exploration is worthwhile because the underlying reason is not curiosity but a commitment to standing alongside, and sharing our resources with, young people, families, and communities under pressure.

Ian Sparks has been in social work since 1971 and has worked in Liverpool, Edinburgh and London. He joined The Children's Society as Social Work Director and was appointed Director in 1986.

LOOKING FORWARD

Paul Henderson

When doing training with social workers on community social work, I became anxious when people began referring to 'projects'. This is because the term denotes finite pieces of work which need not necessarily form part of an organisation's mainstream programme. Projects, one feels, can always be 'added on'.

A reading of the articles in this collection should not give rise to such anxieties for The Children's Society, despite their use of the term 'projects', for these do not appear to be marginal to the Society. Quite the contrary, they are absorbing the energies of staff and committees. Staff are trying new approaches and methods, but they do so with a confidence that the organisation as a whole is behind them. Tensions and uncertainties within the organisation there will be, but that is surely more healthy than being on the sidelines. One senses that there remains energy and commitment at all levels of the Society to explore and develop the community approach.

In the immediate future it is clear that the Society will need to sustain debate and reflection among staff concerning the implications of new ways of working. There are questions which require clarifying and which should be addressed systematically. I wish to select two which the articles point to me:

- the need for a practice theory;
- the issue of accountability.

Practice theory

Nearly ten years ago David Thomas and I, in *Skills in Neighbourhood Work,* identified the emergence of practice theory in community work.[1] We define this as 'know how' and 'know why' propositions. 'Know how' propositions suggest the activities and tasks of community work; their purpose is instructional. 'Know why' propositions contain foundation knowledge as to why people, groups and organisations function in particular ways. Good practice theory integrates the two kinds of propositions, and in recent years there have been several examples of this in community work writing.

Is community social work at the stage of needing similar material: accessible theory which is rooted in fieldworkers' day-to-day practice? The evidence of the articles in this collection suggests a strong need for such practice theory.

Since the publication in 1982 of the Barclay Report[2] its major recommendations on community social work have been examined in various practice and research contexts. There have been some useful results. Yet in my experience, when social work tutors and practitioners are challenged with the question 'what do social workers do when using a community social work framework?' they can draw on relatively few resources. The knowledge and experience of community social work tends to be scattered – it is not unified.

There is a job to be done, therefore, building a practice theory out of the experiences of workers, users and local people – the very experience reflected in the preceding pages. The material needs to have a spine, a set of working principles which relate to each other and from which can be specified the roles required of workers, the tasks they carry out, and the knowledge and resources they must have to do the work effectively. It may be that these will be united most clearly around the idea of process.

The Children's Society is well placed to encourage this kind of development. It has workers who are developing community social work practice. The organisation itself is committed to its development, including a planning system which allows for reflection on practice to take place. In addition, Society staff are in touch with developments in community social work in other settings, and in forums which bring together staff from a number of voluntary and statutory organisations. I am thinking in particular of the community social work networks which exist in some parts of the country. In short, I would encourage the Society to maximise its existing involvement in community social work, to take the next step in work it has developed in this area. Indeed some of its outputs already contribute to the emergence of a practice theory. In addition to Jan Phelan's study there is Joy Adamson and Chris Warren's *Welcome to St Gabriel's Family Centre*,[3] and Bob Holman's *Resourceful Friends – Skills in Community Social Work.*[4]

I am aware that the written work, the continual working for a body of published material which has both depth and breadth, is not seen as a priority by some social workers and community workers. It is perceived as a form of retreat from the realities of a harsh world and of the need for action in response to human suffering. While sympathising with the feeling, I believe it is quite misguided in its conclusion. In western, advanced societies, practitioners underestimate the significance of the written word at their peril. Unless recognition is given to the importance of communicating experiences, making sense of them, and advocating the values and methods contained within them, the experiences are likely to be undervalued. Either they will lose momentum and dwindle, or they will be overtaken by other forms of practice. Realistically, community social work faces this possibility. The wholeness of a profession or an intervention has to be more than the sum of its practice. There has to be an underpinning which can stand up to critical appraisal by those who may not necessarily enthuse about it, and who may need convincing.

Accountability

The goal of achieving local control by community projects is an ambitious one. What is involved in passing over control and responsibility to local people? Undoubtedly it is a very difficult process which has to be planned and worked on over a long timescale. It relates to the issue of evaluation – users of a project and local people need to be involved in the evaluation process, assessing the qualitative difference the project makes to their lives and the neighbourhood.

The Children's Society has to be clear about what it is handing over to local people, what responsibilities they will have and what control – if any – the Society will retain. It will also have to work closely with other local statutory and voluntary agencies: what resources do they have? what links do they have with the neighbourhood where the Society is working?

These questions demonstrate that the Society has to be well prepared if the words 'local control' are to contain substance. For the most part, fieldworkers operate in an organisational system in which they are accountable to regional management, and from there to the national organisation. Arguments for local control imply a shift in the opposite direction: accountability to the neighbourhood and to persons who are involved with a particular project. One has to ask the question, is the Society ready and able to implement such a policy?

It is this question which lies behind the report of the Society's 1986/87 working party on local control. To be able to take up the challenge, the Society needs to be aware of the importance of accountability within community work. At one level this has to do with the autonomy of community groups, the need for them to be free of political or funding constraints and pressures. A group should think twice, for example, before agreeing to have a representative of a funding organisation on its committee as a condition of receiving a grant from that organisation. The ease with which small, often weak, community groups can become incorporated into a powerful organisation is too strong for this issue to be dismissed as activist rhetoric.

Another well-known aspect of accountability in community work concerns the position of community workers. Because of the need for the worker to get close to a group he or she is supporting, the loyalty of the worker can turn increasingly towards a group and away from the employing organisation. Formally, the worker remains accountable to the organisation, but the very essence of effective community work can draw him or her away from it. In other words, the issue of accountability is important not because of any particular personal characteristics of community workers, but because of the nature of the work itself. Experienced community workers might become concerned if the tension between loyalty to a group and accountability to their employing body did *not* arise. They might view its existence as evidence of good practice, not bad.

A third implication of accountability is also focused on workers and relates to the content of work done. It can be put in the form of a question: is the Society prepared for some of its staff to move away from the original remit of a job, from, for example, a responsibility to get activities going at a neighbourhood centre, to addressing the issue of unemployment? A team which followed a philosophy of local control could find itself in such a situation. Local people may identify an issue as a priority and ask the worker to support them, notwithstanding the worker's original job brief. Such a situation could also lead a worker away from a purely neighbourhood base, as he or she might need to work at a town-wide level or on regional planning issues.

The Society may need to ask these questions about accountability in order to move forward with a realistic local control policy. During the next few years we should be looking for a number of ways of working, or practice models, not just one. Each project will undoubtedly develop practice theories and forms of accountability in different ways, and it will be from such variety and richness that the Society will be able to evolve policy.

The articles in this reader show that the Society's projects already have much to contribute to learning about community social work. Other social welfare agencies will benefit from this as well as the Society, and that is always a good benchmark for new forms of practice.

References

[1] Henderson P and Thomas D. *Skills in Neighbourhood Work.* London: Allen and Unwin,1983.

[2] Working Party of National Institute for Social Work. (Chairman: P Barclay). *Social Workers: Their Roles and Tasks.* London: Bedford Square Press, 1982.

[3] Adamson J and Warren C. *Welcome to St Gabriel's Family Centre.* London: The Children's Society, 1983.

[4] Holman R. *Resourceful Friends: Skills in Community Social Work.* London: The Children's Society, 1983.